Go Hard OR Go Home

Bob Foley

Published by Paramount Marketing, LLC

ISBN 978–0-615–39889-1

Paramount Marketing, LLC

11108 W 119thTerrace

Overland Park, KS 66213

rjfoley@kc.rr.com

Printed and bound in the United States of America.

10 9 8 7 6 5 4 3 2 1

Cover design by Gus Nietes, Right Brain Designs, Inc.
Bob Foley picture by Greg Schieszer, Shawnee Mission West HS
Book design and composition by Rick Soldin, Kingsport, TN

To my wife Susan,
who is the love of my life and best friend.
Your love and encouragement over the last twenty-eight years has
allowed me to do what I do and be the man I am.

To my sons, Ryan and Brendan,
who make me so very proud of the men they have become.
I am truly blessed to call myself your father.

To my parents,
Robert (1925–2009) and Mary Ellen (1920–2009).
May you rest in peace.

To Susan's parents,
Donald (1920–1987) and June Sweeney;
I also consider you to be my parents.

To all of my brothers and sisters:
James and his wife Kaye, Ellen and her husband Dick,
my twin sister Deborah, Kevin and his wife Diana,
and Patrick and his wife Jill. I love you all.

Contents

Acknowledgements

Many thanks to all of the basketball coaches I played for during my early years: Coach Dennis Stern, the best basketball coach I ever knew and an even a better person. Coach Thomas Crowe, who helped turn me into me a great shooter. And my college coach, Donald Delaney, who taught me I was not small . . . just not very tall.

To all of my Eastlake North High School teammates who pushed me to work harder so I could achieve the inner goal they never knew I had: To be the best I could be.

To all of my Lakeland teammates who proved that as a group we could achieve so very much without ever caring who got the credit.

To all the players I coached: Believe me, I got more out of the experience than you did. The joy I feel today when I see a former player is something I cannot put into words.

To coach Al McGuire, who personally taught me the fundamentals of free-throw shooting when I was young. May you rest in peace.

To all the basketball coaches I have had the pleasure of working with, including Kevin Pritchard, Reggie King, Rod Seaba, Mike Born, Chad Buchanan, Scott Wedman, Chris Harris and Meadowlark Lemon.

To Jim Stralka, the Vice-President of Purolator Courier who gave me my first national job experience. I worked hard every day so I would not let you down; your leadership skills taught me to stay positive in any situation.

To the management team at Dynamic Drinkware, in particular Jeff Slusarski and Joe Blando: Your efforts are certainly recognized and your Enthusiasm has made our company the highest-quality cup company in the business. I love spending the winter of my career with people so eager to learn and achieve.

To Ron Johnson, the next United States Senator from Wisconsin, for providing me the freedom to start and manage Dynamic Drinkware. You are an outstanding leader and the United States will benefit greatly from your service.

To my friends at Brax LTD, especially Peter Hexter and John Alexander: Without your support this book would not have been possible.

To Dr. James Naismith: Your great game has taught me more than just what happens on the court. The principle of playing together, as a unit, has carried over into my business and personal life as well. This great game has allowed me to travel to different parts of the world and to give back to the great game.

To Meadowlark Lemon, a true basketball legend and one of the most recognized individuals on the planet. Through good, clean, old-time family fun you have brought smiles and joy to people all over the world. You are truly a remarkable person and I am a better person for knowing you.

To Frank Martin, men's basketball head coach at Kansas State University, one of the most intense college coaches in the country. You lead by example and compete as hard as any person in their chosen profession. You truly care for your players and staff, and I admire your loyalty and devotion to the people who have helped make you such a success.

To Desmond Hague, President and CEO of Centerplate. Meeting you and working with your group has made me a better leader. You are a great example of how to bring the 3 E's: Effort, Emotion Enthusiasm. With Des, you get what you see—and what you see is always spectacular.

To Ed Eppley, one of the most intelligent people I have ever met and without question the very best business and sales trainer alive.

To Bill Zirger, my daily mentor. I tip my hat to your years of incredible success in the sales game.

To my brothers and sisters on my wife's side of the family: Terry and Becky, Cyndi and Stephen, Kathy and Michael (1943–2004), Tim and Michelle. We are sorry we live so far away.

To all the wonderful people that I have worked for and associates that have help me grow by their knowledge, spirit and enthusiasm, plus all the wonderful customers I have had the privilege to call on, work with and manage: I have truly enjoyed every single one of you.

To Jeff Haden of BlackBird Media, you have been spectacular and your guidance during this book project has been most professional and second to none.

Foreword

I look for the best. I don't settle for second-best. I never have. I do everything I can to surround myself with the best people.

That's how I played with superstars like—to name just a few—Wilt Chamberlain, Marques Haynes, Connie Hawkins, and Curly Neal. That's how I worked with people like Johnny Carson and Bill Cosby. If you want to be the best, surround yourself with the best.

Like my friend Bob Foley.

I am probably best known for my basketball career with the Harlem Globetrotters and later my own team, the Bucketeers. Other people may know me from my career in movies and television, and the dozens of television commercials I appeared in. Still others may know me due to the books I've written and the music I've recorded.

I'm proud of all my accomplishments. I've been fortunate enough to help entertain millions of people. But accomplishments are fleeting. The difference we make in another person's life lasts forever.

But we only make a difference when we give our utmost to whatever we do.

When I started with the Globetrotters we traveled constantly. We averaged over 300 games a year. I can't say it was easy. We traveled by plane, by bus, by car...sometimes I felt we spent more time moving than we did standing still. People still ask me if it was tough to give it my best on the court, night after night after night.

It wasn't tough at all. When I walked on the court I knew there were people in the crowd who had been saving money for weeks or months in order to buy tickets to the game. Families today might save money all year to go on vacation; back then, in some of the small towns we visited, many of the folks were so poor they had to save up their money just to come see us.

When I looked in the crowd and saw people who were making huge sacrifices to come to the game, it was easy to give my best. Talk about inspiring. I was honored. I felt truly blessed. Those folks gave it their all to come see us play—I gave it my all so they would get my best in return.

What do you do best? Lots of people do a number of things well. I was an all-state good football player when I was young, but I knew basketball created the best opportunities. So I put basketball first and my goal of becoming a Globetrotter. I put in the thousands of hours of work it took to succeed.

Like Bob says, I *needed* to succeed. Failure was not an option. So I did the work.

Fortunately I found all the support I needed along the way. All these years later I still remember teachers like Mrs. Cotton, Mr. Bryant and Coach Earl Jackson. They helped me take what I was taught, put it in a package, and pull it all together.

Even today I try to follow a simple premise:

What you lack, seek.

Recognize your strengths and weaknesses, work to make your weaknesses become strengths, with these improvements you will become a better person.

Later I turned a page in my life and became an ordained minister. I still love basketball, but my main focus is on helping people through our ministry. We work with individuals, families, children…whoever needs us. We produce a nationally-televised weekly ministry. We recently started a distance learning institution for kids. We developed a co-ed sports camp to offer children alternatives to substance abuse. We work with youths in prison. We go where we are needed.

We try to make a difference.

And we give it our all.

The jump from basketball to the ministry may seem large, but it is not. I haven't changed. I just turned a page.

That's what life is all about.

Bob Foley hasn't changed either. For all the years I've known him, Bob has done things the right way. Bob knows how to win—the right way. He does all the little things that make a person successful. Achieving success isn't complicated: Achieving success is based on focus, dedication, and a willingness to work as hard as you can to reach your dreams.

That's life. When you turn a page and step off in another direction, whatever you do, give it your all. Do your best.

Surround yourself with the best.

I do. That's why Bob and I are friends.

—**Meadowlark Lemon**

Introduction

It says a lot about a person when you do something bad to them and they repay you with honor. Like in this case: I almost got Bob Foley fired from a job he was about to be offered, and yet he still asked me write the Introduction for this book.

First a little background. Since I've known him, Bob has always taken every opportunity to embarrass me in public, whenever and wherever possible. I try to return the favor, but I have to admit Bob is ahead on both the quantity and quality of pranks.

Except for this one time....

One day I answered the phone and the caller said, "We are considering Bob Foley for the head coaching position of our professional basketball team. He listed you as a reference. Can you tell me a little about Bob?"

I assumed the call was a prank. I figured Bob had one of his friends call to play some kind of joke on me. I thought,

"Okay...I'm not falling for it this time." So I decided to have a little fun.

I said, "Bob Foley? You are thinking about hiring Bob Foley? Are you crazy? I can't believe anyone would consider hiring Bob. He has horrible people skills. He talks a good game but his basketball knowledge is limited at best. And if that's not bad enough, there's the substance abuse problem to consider..."

The caller was shocked. He stumbled and stammered and asked a few more questions. I could tell he was stunned, so I assumed he wasn't able to think fast enough on his feet to turn the prank back on me. I ended the call by saying, "I wouldn't consider hiring a bum like Bob Foley in a million years," and hung up pretty darned satisfied with my performance. For once I had side-stepped a practical joke.

Then Bob called. "What did you say to them!" he exclaimed.

I tried to act innocent. "Gee, Bob, I don't know. I just told the truth about you."

"You must have said something," Bob said. "They had all but offered me the job. They said calling you was just a formality. They just wanted to conduct a brief reference check before formally extending the offer."

Wow, I thought, Bob is really sticking with his joke. "I don't know, Bob," I said. "What did they tell you about the call?"

"They said, and I'm quoting here, 'Bob, I don't think we can offer you the job after all. On paper and in person you look great, but your references really don't match up with what we thought we were getting.'"

As it turns out I had actually spoken to the president of a basketball team in Kansas City. Bob had been about to get the job...until I lit him up, that is. Immediately after speaking with me they pulled Bob out of the running for the job.

Even though I felt bad (okay, I only felt bad for about thirty seconds), my response to the initial call could not have been more on target. While I didn't know the caller was legitimate, I still managed to push all the right buttons. I denigrated Bob's basketball knowledge. I called his leadership ability into question. I said he was a terrible team player. Best of all—or worst of all—I said Bob had a substance abuse issue. Sure, a substance abuse problem is problematic at best...but the team had just let the previous coach go due after he was arrested for a DUI. They were understandably sensitive to even a hint of a substance abuse issue. Perfect!

Except Bob was now out the running for a job he really wanted—and was perfect for.

So Bob called them back and explained the situation. He described our history of practical jokes, let them know I was unaware they would be calling, and asked if they would give me a chance to speak truthfully to his qualifications, background, and suitability for the job.

They were kind enough to call me again, and I was honest and forthright. Bob got the job.

And I got Bob back, just a little, for all the jokes he has played on me.

If you know Bob you quickly begin to appreciate his sense of humor, loyalty, love of 60's rock and practical jokes (especially ones he gets to pull), his dedication to his family, and his amazing network of friends and contacts, not just in sports but in business and in life.

I've known Bob and his wife Susan for over thirty years. During that time I've watched Bob rise in the business ranks while at the same time successfully pursue his passion for coaching. Bob has an incredible knack for taking a group of talent and molding them into something better than they were—or even thought they could be.

That Bob has been able to accomplish this on two different stages is testimony to his mental toughness, talent and drive to succeed. This book will help you better understand how anyone who wants to rise to "the next level" can do so.

As you read this book you'll get to know the Bob Foley I know, respect and love. And my guess is you, like me, will be a better person for it.

— **Ed Eppley, Executive Vice President,**
Tyson Eppley Management

One

32220 Lake Shore Boulevard

M uch of what I know about life—and by extension, about business—I learned by the time I was fourteen years old.

Granted, I've learned a lot more over the years. I graduated from a great college, worked in a variety of management, leadership, sales, and executive positions, and coached basketball at every level from youth to professional. As I like to say, I've earned my gray hair and I'm proud of it. Gray hair is not just an automatic by-product of aging. Gray hair can also be a tangible symbol of knowledge, wisdom, and hard-earned experience.

So yes, I've learned a lot since I was fourteen. But some lessons stick with you and shape the person you become, no matter your age or your background. In fact, that's true even if your childhood is anything but typical.

Take my childhood, for instance. I was incredibly fortunate: While my family lived at 32220 Lake Shore Boulevard in Willowick, a suburb of Cleveland, Ohio, I lived much of my formative years at Municipal Stadium.

I also lived at Yankee Stadium.

And I also lived at the Boston Garden.

You see, each evening at 6:00 p.m. our family sat down at the kitchen table for dinner. Every meal was a sell-out: My father and mother, three brothers, and two sisters ate a wonderful meal from the best restaurant in town, Mary Ellen's Kitchen. (Mary Ellen, incidentally, was our mom.)

But we didn't just enjoy a meal. My father also conducted what we thought of, in a good way, as "quiz time." He asked us questions about history, math, science, and current events that provided a springboard to a variety of topics and far-ranging conversations. The food was fabulous and the discussions were even better. Eating dinner was often the highlight of my day, and as I look back, those times helped create the foundation for a real sense of family togetherness. When I think of my childhood years, I think of sitting at the table with my family.

I miss that table.

After dinner one of us kids had clean-up duty. Wednesday was my night to do the dishes. My mother and father would linger at the kitchen table, enjoying a cup of coffee but more importantly a little quiet time together. (In a house with six children, quiet time was at a premium.)

While they sat talking softly, they could look out the back window and watch me shooting baskets in our backyard. We lived in the snowbelt near Lake Erie, but not even bitter cold, ice, and snow could stop me from playing ball after dinner. I'm sure they enjoyed watching their little boy play...but I'm also sure they had no idea I was not their little boy and I wasn't really in the backyard.

What my parents didn't know is that I was far away. They and I were in different worlds. My parents were still in the kitchen, but I was in the Boston Garden making game-winning shot after game-winning shot.

When spring arrived the front yard turned into Yankee Stadium and I alternated between being Mickey Mantle and Whitey Ford. I hit from both sides of the plate with equal power. I had base-running speed every player envied. As a pitcher I never had less than twelve strikeouts, and during one "season" alone I threw six no-hitters. (Take *that*, Nolan Ryan.) Almost every game ended with me hitting a bases loaded, ninth inning, three-and-two-count, walk-off home run to win the game.

When summer turned to fall, I moved to Cleveland's Municipal Stadium, gaining over 1,000 yards a season and catching game-winning, toe-dragging, inbounds by a fraction touchdown passes.

That's why I was so fortunate. 32220 Lake Shore Blvd was truly a magical place. As a child I dreamed big dreams. I played in big games and made big shots, ran for game-winning touchdowns, hit game-winning home runs...it seemed so natural and so real.

I hope that as a child you dreamed big dreams and were able to chase your dreams to happiness. If you didn't—it's not too late.

I was also fortunate in other ways. The city of Willowick had a great recreation department, offering organized baseball, football, and swimming. At age nine you could enter the city's organized sports programs. But an age limit didn't mean you had to wait to begin your athletic career or confine yourself to organized sports: For example, during the summer my friends and I played pickup baseball games at the local Roosevelt School field. Every day I was on the school yard. We played hard and we played a lot: The only time we went home was for a quick lunch and then for dinner. (As you can guess, I hated when it rained.)

When I turned nine I was finally able to join the recreation program. On the days I had an organized baseball game at Dudley Park I would almost tremble with anticipation, but my excitement didn't translate to results. My first year playing recreation baseball was, to be honest, a disaster.

Why? In spite of my school yard, pick-up game heroics, and in spite of my days patrolling the outfield in Yankee Stadium, during organized games I could not catch a ball either in the air or on the ground. As a hitter, only once did I manage to make contact with a pitch, dribbling a slow-rolling ground ball into foul territory. My batting average was an amazing .000. (I achieved perfection, but not in a good way.)

I was a terrible player. But I did excel in one way.

I was a world-class trash talker.

I yelled at batters. I told them they couldn't hit. I told them they stunk. I told them they couldn't catch. I heckled batters who swung and missed. I heckled fielders who booted ground balls or made throwing errors.

Never mind that I couldn't hit or play the field worth a darn. There I was: The worst-producing player on the field yet also the player with the biggest mouth.

I can only imagine the embarrassment my parents felt. They weren't embarrassed by my poor play; they were embarrassed by my attitude and my behavior. In fact they were so embarrassed they stopped coming to my games at all. After the third game they dropped me off before games and picked me up afterwards.

In the process I learned a big lesson: Let your game do the talking. (I know what you're thinking. That's a lesson a number of professional athletes could benefit from learning.) The second year I was still just as excited, but by then I was mentally ready to play organized baseball.

Even so, my family decided not to attend the first game.

As I look back I certainly understand my parents' logic and point of view, but it's too bad they weren't there for the first game of my second season. I hit three home runs and pitched a no-hitter. When I jumped in the car after the game I told my family about my exploits but they thought I was, well, full of it, and they didn't believe me. (Looking back, I wouldn't have believed me, either.) After the second game I asked our coach to write a note to my parents so they would realize I really was playing like a star. After the second game my parents attended every baseball game that I played, all the way from little league through high school.

The rest of that season was a lot of fun. We won the championship and I was selected for the all-star team.

But even if the phrase, "Let your game do the talking," is one I learned to live my life by, it's not the biggest lesson I learned in my early years.

At age thirteen I was introduced to the game of basketball, and I quickly shifted baseball to the back burner. My sports days were consumed with playing basketball, even though I was one of the smallest guys in my school class. I never thought of height as a positive or a negative per se—I was just who I was. My goals were to play high school basketball, be all-city and all-conference, and then play college basketball.

Like I said, I dreamed big dreams.

The varsity basketball coach at Eastlake North High School was a wonderful man named Tom Crowe. Coach Crowe had been the head coach for over twenty-five years and had earned the respect of each and every one of his players and from the community as a whole. If you played basketball in my town you knew Coach Crowe—and you wanted to play for him.

A major turning point in my life occurred when Coach Crowe spoke to my freshman team. When he finished speaking he asked if we had any questions. Since I was by far the smallest player on the team, and one of the least experienced (and skilled), I asked him what I needed to do to be able to make the varsity basketball team at Eastlake North High School so I could play for him.

To his credit he took my question seriously. He also didn't sugar-coat his answer. Instead of telling me what I might have *wanted* to hear, he told me what I *needed* to hear.

First he mentioned my lack of height and asked how tall my father was. His assessment was straightforward: Based on my physical attributes—or lack thereof—I would have to be a point guard. He said his point guards must be able to handle ball pressure, make good decisions with the ball, be able to run, run, and run some more, and to not only be a good shooter but to be a great shooter—especially a great free-throw shooter.

His reasoning was simple: When the game is on the line and time is running out, when defense and rebounding are critical, for a small point guard to stay on the floor he must be the best free-throw shooter on the team. (Take Shaquille O'Neal, a notoriously poor free-throw shooter: Would you want him on the floor at the end of a tight game when the other team is likely to foul? I wouldn't. He's not likely to make his free throws.)

That's all I needed to hear. I didn't dwell on my shortcomings. I focused on the positives and on the clear direction he provided. I walked away knowing that if I could run, run, and run some more, handle the ball well, make great decisions, and be the best free-throw shooter on the team, there was a place for me on Coach Crowe's squad. The future seemed simple: Just work on the areas of the game Coach Crowe pointed out, master the point guard position, and I could achieve my dreams.

More good fortune came my way. Before I was old enough to play varsity basketball I benefited from great coaching. The freshman coach, Dennis Stern, was one of the very best basketball coaches I would ever play for. Even though I was a 5'4" seventh grader, Coach Stern made me the starting point guard on his freshman team. However, I had to earn that position and that responsibility. Coach Stern not only taught me basketball—he also showed me how to work hard to be successful in the classroom, too.

And he also taught me that hard work doesn't have an end date. Our official basketball season began in mid-November and ended in mid-March. But as Coach Stern said, "Mid-March through mid-October is really when *players* are made."

If that doesn't make sense, think of it in business terms: What makes you successful in a particular job isn't what you learn when you *have* the job, it's what you learn when you *don't* have the position—*yet*. Then, what allows you to continue to be successful isn't just what you do *during* working hours; it's what you do *outside* of working hours to continue to develop your skills, your knowledge, and your abilities.

What did *I* do to make myself a better player? In the summer my normal routine was to get up by 8 a.m., shoot no less than 250 free throws, perform a variety of ball-handling drills with each hand, and work on individual offensive moves. After lunch I went to the local playground to join in pickup baseball games. After dinner I went to Dudley Park to watch the high school guys play basketball so I could pick up their offensive and defensive moves. I also tried to join in. About half the time I would manage to get into games, trying to play with much bigger, stronger, and more mature high school players. Coach Stern played in those games as well, and while I didn't realize it at the time he was watching me as closely as I watched him. I noticed and was incredibly impressed by his work ethic, kindness, and solid fundamentals. I walked home every night dreaming of being able to play like Coach Stern.

In turn he noticed my passion for the game and my desire to improve, so he went out of his way to help me. In the middle of that summer he noticed my shooting had improved, and he gave me a shooting device that would change not only my basketball career but my outlook on life. Here's the deal: On a regulation basketball goal, two balls will fit inside the rim at the same time. (It's a tight squeeze, but they will fit.) Coach Stern gave me a smaller rim that attached to and fit inside a regulation rim; once in place, only one ball would fit. I was so excited about the new rim—and about the fact Coach Stern had not only noticed me but had gone out of his way to help me—that I rushed home to attach it to my rim in the backyard.

Excitement was quickly replaced by frustration. The smaller rim created a huge challenge for me. At first I struggled to make layups, and ten-foot jumpers were almost impossible to make.

I kept trying, though, and after a time realized that no amount of "trying harder" was going to make me better. What I was doing simply wasn't working.

So I took a step back. After a few weeks—yes, I stuck with it that long—I realized that in order to make shots on a smaller rim, I needed to shoot the ball higher, putting more arc on the ball. I know that sounds simple, and it is. Think about the geometry. Take a dinner plate and look straight down on it. When you look squarely at the plate, its diameter appears to be large. Now pick the plate up and tilt it slightly away from you. The more you tilt the plate, the smaller the diameter appears to be.

That's what happens in basketball. A relatively flat arcing shot has to be almost perfect in order to go in; in theory, if you could stand almost directly under the basket and shoot the ball almost straight up, when it comes down your shot has a much better chance of going in since two balls will fit in a standard rim. The rim itself doesn't change, but the "available" angle changes depending on the arc of your shot. Shoot flat and you better be perfect; shoot higher and you automatically increase your margin of error.

Proving that my father's "quiz time" exercises weren't in vain, geometry became my friend when I realized I needed to change my overall approach to shooting. To be successful on the small rim—and by extension on a regulation rim—I needed to shoot the ball higher and create more arc on my shots.

Soon I was able to make about half of the free throws I attempted on the smaller rim. A little success made me work even harder. I started shooting 500 free throws a day instead of 250. And I didn't stop there: After my 500th shot, I would not stop until I made ten shots in a row; if I made nine and missed the tenth, I had to start over.

I worked all summer and by the time I went back to school in September as a fourteen year-old, I was making 70% of my free-throws on the smaller rim. And I realized that if you really want to improve, challenge yourself to do what may seem impossible. If you stick with it, work hard, and devote not just your energy but also your intelligence to the challenge...you will find a way.

So what did I know by the time I was fourteen?

- I learned to tell people what they *need* to hear, not what they *want* to hear.

- I learned that finding people who believe in you makes all the difference.

- I learned that if you have a plan, and you work that plan, you can achieve your dreams.

- I learned that good luck and fortune are important, but what matters is what you *do* with the opportunities you receive.

- I learned challenges are actually exciting opportunities. Because when you take a step back, assess the situation, and find ways your intelligence, experience, and most importantly hard work can help you overcome the immediate obstacle...you also become a better person in the process.

When I was fourteen I began to learn how to earn my gray hair—and I haven't looked back.

I've also never forgotten the impact made by Coach Crowe, Coach Stern, and the dozens of other people who have helped me along the way. None of us do anything worthwhile on our own.

I'm living proof.

That's my goal: Hopefully you can learn from what I have learned—and from what other people have taught me—to not only help you reach *your* dreams, but so you can help others reach *their* dreams, too.

What's the first step? The first step is actually to take a step back...and know the history of what you do.

Two

Know What You Do

We live in a "tomorrow" society. The pace of change, the speed of technological advancements, the incredible breakthroughs in science, medicine, and even business cause us to look forward. In a way that certainly makes sense—after all, what you do today and what you will do tomorrow is in many ways more important than what you did yesterday.

But as a business—and personal—philosophy, only looking forward is a mistake.

Why? In business or in any other profession, whether it's teaching, public service, sports, or any other industry, you should understand the "beginning." Not just the beginning of your organization, but the beginning of your industry. I call it "knowing the history of what you do."

Knowing the history of what you do pays off.

Take me, for example. Aside from my family, my two big "things" are basketball and cups.

Let's start with basketball. When I go to basketball camps I naturally talk about basketball. When I speak to business groups I also talk about basketball. I *always* talk about basketball. You can take the old coach out of the game but you can never take the game out of the old coach. Even though I don't actively coach any teams today, I still consider myself a basketball coach and at heart a basketball guy. That will never change.

Kids and adults are extremely attentive when I talk about the history of basketball. It's an amazing game. Invented by Dr. James Naismith in Springfield, Massachusetts in 1891, incredibly enough by 1894 basketball was played in China. (Imagine: Pre-telephone, pre-television, pre-Internet…and basketball spread around the world in just three short years.)

Dr. Naismith clearly knew what he was doing. Basketball is based on thirteen original rules, and those thirteen rules are still in effect, with great results: Today, 17,800 boys and girls will play high school basketball this season in the United States alone.

Why is basketball so popular? One, it's a game that can be played with ten people, six people, four people, two people…you can even play by yourself. (I'm living proof of that: I logged thousands of hours playing basketball by myself in my backyard, on playgrounds, and in gyms. Try spending that much time alone playing, say, baseball or football.)

Two, basketball can be played by players of all sizes and shapes, of widely different abilities, boys and girls separately or together, and by players of any age. It's a universal game. A good friend of mine is seventy-six years old and still plays three nights a week. His game is based on playing good defense, making intelligent passes, and spotting up to shoot threes. Over the years he has continually adapted his game to suit his physical abilities and as a result he still contributes...and most importantly he still has fun.

Now take plastic cups.

Plastic took off in the 1960s. The plastics industry was kick-started by the space program—they needed strong, easily shaped, lightweight materials for building spacecrafts. (In fact, the space program is responsible for hundreds if not thousands of innovations and technological advancements that we continue to benefit from today.)

During that time Jim Schwartzburg was the owner of a company based in Lawrence, Kansas called Packer Plastics. They made plastic flower pots. One of their larger customers was Hallmark (the greeting card people), and Packer Plastics made a 22-ounce fluted flower pot for Hallmark. For whatever reason Hallmark did not order that particular flower pot for a couple of years, so in 1968 Jim asked Hallmark if he could plug the holes in the bottom and sell the flower pots as cups. (If you think about it, Packer Plastics didn't have to ask for Hallmark's permission—but it was good business and smart customer relations to do so.)

Plugging the holes in the bottom turned flower pots into cups, which was great…but Packer Plastics still didn't have a customer for those cups. Jim asked one of his sales reps to approach the University of Kansas to see if they wanted to sell printed plastic cups at football games. The person in charge of concession sales at the University of Kansas said, "Why should I pay you for cups? Pepsi gives me cups for free."

Good question. The sales rep replied, "Well, if I don't get this order I may have to sell hot dogs for you at halftime in order to pay my bills." I'm sure he said a lot more, and to make a long story short the concession manager agreed to order 500 white plastic cups with the Jayhawks logo printed in blue on the side of the cup. (Based on the small size of the order he clearly planned to limit his losses if the cups were a bust.)

At the game the cups sold out in minutes. As the sales rep later explained, "You would have thought the Beatles had arrived and were at the concession stand." The concession manager ordered 5,000 cups for the next game…and a new industry was born. The Kansas Jayhawks plastic cup was the first printed concessions plastic cup in the world.

Today one of those cups is on display in the Smithsonian.

For the next fifteen years plastic cups were sold throughout the United States and across the world. Sales were solid but the industry grew static: No innovation, no change. Big users—especially fast food companies like McDonalds, Taco Bell, Burger King, etc—shifted away from plastic collectible cups and moved to semi-disposable thermoform cups using dry offset printing. The cups looked fairly good, but as was printed on the bottom of the cup, were designed for one-time use only. From the companies' point of view moving to a less expensive disposable cup made sense: Costs were lower, print quality was roughly similar, and besides, customers had grown less interested in purchasing collector cups.

Five years later I came into the cup world and immediately realized technological advances in the printing industry could be applied to plastic cup manufacturing. I saw the opportunity to produce in-mold label cups resulting in better decorations, better graphics, and significantly higher print quality.

But even though we were able to produce a higher quality product, I can't say there was no resistance to our cups, at least not at first. Our cups cost more. We had to prove to potential customers that *their* customers would be willing to pay a premium for a beverage contained in a high-quality collector cup.

Delivering that proof turned out to be easy. For example, we created a cup for one of the leading universities in the Southeastern Conference (SEC); based on their beverage sales experience they estimated they would sell 85,000 collector cups over the course of a football season. Midway through the second game all 85,000 cups had sold out. (They eventually sold over 325,000 cups based on that first design alone.)

Results like those helped us develop a track record of retail and concession sales that proved our customers could sell more beverages using our collector cups. Years of data proves consumers are eager to purchase a better-designed, better-printed collector cup.

Think about it this way: In any business you sell a product or service, but what you really provide is a *benefit*. A soft drink, in the beverage world, is a product. You can drink a soft drink from a bottle, a can, a cup...the soft drink itself is the same but the "method of delivery" is different and as a result the benefits can be different. (By the way, research shows most people, given the choice, prefer to drink from a cup.)

If you are in the concessions (or restaurant or retail) business and you sell a soft drink in a bottle or a can, your profits are relatively low because you must buy that bottle or can from a distributor. You make pennies on the sale of each unit, if that much. When you sell soft drinks in cups, you only pay for the syrup but you can still charge consumers the same price for the drink. Syrup is relatively inexpensive (you don't want to know just how "relatively inexpensive" syrup is) so you can avoid distributor markups and enjoy higher profits. In short, you can make a lot more pennies on each unit you sell.

Again, the product is the same, but the method of delivery is different.

Granted, at most sporting events today buying a bottle or can is impossible, so the discussion of cans and bottles is somewhat moot. Bottles and cans, if thrown, turn into dangerous weapons. (Try buying a bottled beverage at a soccer game in Europe—you can't.)

That's true in the U.S. as well, for reasons I know first-hand. I particularly remember a basketball game I played in college against West Virginia in the pre-shot clock days. We held the ball and went in at halftime with the score 7–5. In the second half we opened up the game and Jeff LaCava, our 6'5" forward, hit a game-winning 15-foot shot from the corner to give us a 44–43 victory. Running through the tunnel on the way to the locker room fans threw food, pennies, and bottles at us. Some even dumped garbage cans on us as we ran by. So if you ask me if I mind that bottles and cans have been banned at most sporting events, I'll say I no—and not just because it's good for my business.

Of course, in order to sell soft drinks in cups, you need cups. That's where we come in.

Our first customer was a major motion picture studio. We created a theater cup based on a movie.

I can't say it was an easy sell. First we focused on quality. We asked, "How much do you spend on good will? How much do you spend to ensure your logos are printed correctly? What do you do to protect your image and your brand?"

Then we focused on concession sales and how the studio's current suppliers were not able to meet their quality expectations. We proved we could produce a picture-perfect cup that not only protected the studio's brand but extended it onto new platforms and media. We really had to prove ourselves, but the results were worth it: The cups took off, the studio and the theaters who sold more drinks (at higher profit margins) were delighted, and we haven't looked back.

By the way: The happiest person was not the concession manager, studio owner, theatre owner or cup sales person. The happiest person was the custodian who cleans the theatre after the last showing ended. There were no plastic collector cups to pick up and throw away. The cups were truly collector items and moviegoers took them all home. Some wanted to collect the cups, others simply wanted to re-use them, and some saw them as conversation-starters. Whatever the reason behind each purchase, all the cups went home with their buyers.

Today we have the lion's share of the plastic collector cup market. We may not sell the cheapest cup, but we absolutely provide the _best-priced_ cup on the market.

How can I claim we sell the best-priced cup?

One, as we like to say, we do common things uncommonly well. We deliver on time. We answer phone calls. We return emails. We over-serve our customers. If we can't meet your delivery needs, we won't take your order because sometimes the best deal is no deal at all. (I'd rather tell you today that I can't meet your needs than accept an order only to fail later—the end result, failing to meet your needs, is the same, but the outcome in terms of customer relationships is dramatically different.)

We also produce a better quality cup, and we can prove it. We frequently run focus tests. We go to malls, fast food restaurants, or convenience stores and set up displays. We put ten cups on the table: Eight printed using dry-offset techniques and two using our lenticular (a fancy term referring to printing that creates the illusion of depth), in-mold label technology. We then ask customers to take the cup they want.

Well over 90% take our cups instead of a dry-offset cup. Our cups look better. Even though customers may not understand the technology—or the history of what we do—people instinctively recognize and respond to quality.

Plus, we help our customers develop a series of cups, not simply a one-off cup. Series sell better. While we could produce, say, a Richard Petty cup, we've found that producing a series of NASCAR driver cups will generate significantly higher sales. People love collecting items they feel are valuable. People love collecting items with significance in their lives.

For example, some years ago we produced a series of cups for University of Alabama football games. Because we can do neat things with color we were able to create retro-themed cups. Instead of featuring current players, we developed cups highlighting Crimson Tide legends from the past: Joe Namath, Bear Bryant, Lee Roy Jordan, Ken Stabler...the cups were wildly popular with both young and old fans. Younger fans enjoyed learning about legends from the past, and older fans enjoyed talking about the players they knew and loved.

Picture a father and son at a game, the father telling stories about past players...when that happens, a cup is no longer just a cup. The cup becomes a window into the past and a bridge to connect generations.

Most importantly, we recognize—and in fact thrive—on the fact we are not in a commodity business. When you sell a commodity it's tough to win, especially long-term, because someone can always come in and beat you on price even if doing so eventually puts them out of business. When you sell commodities the only way to win business is on price. Quality matters, of course, but the bottom line price is everything.

Sometimes potential customers say, "We buy a dry-offset cup and it costs less than your cup. Why should I buy your cup?" It's a fair question. My standard reply is to say, "I understand. Here's what you should do: Go to your current supplier and ask them to match our quality."

I know they can't.

A lot of people know everything about price, but nothing about value. Value transcends commodity pricing because value is based on a lot more than cost.

Think about it in automotive terms. In the 1970s Japanese auto manufacturers entered the U.S. market. Detroit didn't take the competition seriously, much to their eventual chagrin. Datsun (now called Nissan) was first, quickly followed by Toyota and Honda. All three companies originally took the commodity approach: In effect they said to consumers, "Why pay $15,000 for a car when you can buy the same quality car for $12,000?" They competed on a commodity basis and used price to win customers. The quality was similar (or sadly, often better) and the price was lower.

That's the commodity pricing model in a nutshell.

After winning customers based on lower prices, Japanese automakers took the next step. Overcoming the resistance to buying a foreign car was significant; once initial resistance was conquered Japanese automakers were able to introduce a more upscale line of cars. For example, Toyota introduced its Lexus line and Honda introduced Acura. In short, they leveraged their current customers to sell more expensive (and profitable) cars.

Here's the Japanese automaker strategy in a nutshell: Overcome customer purchase hesitation by competing effectively on a commodity basis, then build on that customer base to sell more expensive and more profitable cars.

If you feel the Japanese developed a new business strategy...you are wrong. General Motors became the largest auto manufacturer in the world by following the same simple strategy, and companies like Ford followed suit. For years the GM auto line and sales strategy was based on "moving" customers through different price levels as they aged and became more affluent: GM built entry-level cars, mid-range cars, luxury cars...all under the assumption that customers would stick with GM cars for life.

And for decades that strategy worked...until Japanese companies came along and executed the same strategy more effectively.

The quality of Japanese cars—this is a key factor—was relatively high, so the value proposition made sense to consumers. Over time consumers believed Japanese cars would last longer than American-made cars. Consumers were willing to pay a premium for perceived quality. People buy quality—otherwise why would someone pay $45,000 for a car when they can buy a "similar" car for $25,000? The difference is in the quality and the value proposition the consumer feels they receive for the money they spend.

People are, and will always be, willing to pay for quality.

The same thing happened with the first collector cups sold at the Kansas football game. Customers bought quality. The cup business went upscale.

Japanese automakers followed the same route. Over time they went upscale. As I was thinking about the history of the automotive industry, I realized we could use the same tactics where plastic cups were concerned. It seems simple today, but I knew I could take what occurred in the automotive industry and transfer the concept to cups. Sure, as a company we could have entered the dry-offset cup business, but then we would only have been able to compete on price. Instead, since we provide more than just a commodity item, we are not forced to be the low-cost provider because we offer a dramatically different value proposition to our customers.

Keep in mind we do occasionally lose deals based on price considerations. So too does any good manufacturer. Sometimes the customer simply cannot afford to purchase the product you sell. That's okay. Someday they may, and you'll be there.

But we don't lose deals based on value, and that's an important distinction. To show you how, let's work through some simple calculations. (Keep in mind these are hypothetical numbers, not actual costs, margins, or prices, plus I'm intentionally keeping the math simple.)

Say you sell soft drinks. You sell a 20-ounce drink for $1.00. The soft drink itself costs you .20 and your cups cost .10 each. So, you make .70 per sale (I'm purposely not factoring in labor and other costs, of course.) On an average day you sell 1,000 drinks for gross revenues of $1,000 and net profits of $700.

Now say you sell a 20-ounce drink in a plastic collector cup. The cost of the soft drink is the same, but the cups cost you .30 each. That's okay, because customers love the cups and are willing to pay a premium, allowing you to sell those drinks for $1.60 each. And not only that, but more customers want your drinks. They don't just want a soft drink—they want the cup, too. Instead of selling an average of 1,000 per day, you sell 1,500 per day.

So what happens? Your costs are up but so are your revenues. You now net $1.20 per sale instead of .70, and you also make 500 more sales per day. Your gross revenue rises to $2,400 and your net profits increase to $1,800.

So, would you provide customers with the collector cup option based on those kinds of results? Of course, and our customers do. Our cups may not be the cheapest on the market, but they are the best-priced and offer the best value proposition to our customers.

Success is great, but we don't rest on our laurels. Today we're working on new decorations, new product styles, and new manufacturing methods—if we don't, someone will eventually come along and beat us.

Now, I know what you might be thinking. "Our business is different," you may say. "What you did might work in plastic cups, but it won't work for us."

Not true. Knowing the history of what you do pays dividends in any business.

Don't believe me? Let's talk about a company widely-regarded as one of the most innovative companies in the world: Apple. Apple loves to say they create revolutionary products, and in some ways they are right—but in other ways they are wrong. How can I say that?

Take the iPod. Portable music players and even portable mp3 players existed before the iPod came along. Or take the iPhone. Smart phones predate the iPhone. What Apple does best is take existing technologies and existing customer preferences and rework them to solve existing problems and better serve consumer needs.

In short, Apple doesn't create "new." Apple takes "what is" and makes "what is" a whole lot better.

Here's a quick example. Microsoft developed a Windows-based computer tablet back in 2001 to great fanfare but poor results: The interface was clunky, the operating system was buggy at best, developers weren't able to develop applications for the device, and even Microsoft software like Word and Excel was not made available to users. Some years later, Apple realized the problem did not lie in the tablet concept itself but in the *execution* of the tablet concept. So Apple set out to execute better. Developing an effective operating system and interface was a slam-dunk, since Apple had already solved those problems on the iPhone (and knew customers loved those solutions.) Developers had already created thousands of applications for iPods and iPhones, so programs were not an issue (and Apple knew consumers love apps.)

That's why the iPad, for all its "revolutionary" technology, is not a new device or a new innovation. The iPad is a better-executed version of an old idea. The result combines lots of different technologies and strategies to match customer preferences and exceed customer expectations.

But even though the iPad isn't "new," Apple sold two million iPads in the first sixty days. First they looked at what once was, then at what now is...and then looked forward to what could be.

When you are in business—regardless of the industry—take a step back and learn about the history of your business and your industry. Where you are going is important, but where you have been is incredibly powerful information you can use to guide you on the journey to where you are going.

You also may be surprised to learn that your customers, your manufacturers, your vendors, and your employees are all interested in the past. History is powerful—if you let it be.

Why? Many people want to get to the destination without making the trip—knowing the history of what you do is a key part of taking the trip.

And along the way you may identify opportunities to turn past mistakes into future successes. By definition winners are successful; let's look at two main philosophies that create winners—and success.

Three

Building Winning Teams

Life can often seem complicated, but life is fairly simple if you step back and think about it.

Take raising kids. Thousands of books have been written about child-raising techniques, strategies, and philosophies, but to my wife and me, raising children boiled down to a simple premise: We wanted our kids to be good citizens, to be caring, to be compassionate, and to give back. When we had decisions to make, we considered those goals—and solving potentially sticky situations suddenly seemed a lot simpler.

I have two main philosophies I follow in business and in basketball. (Remember, you can't take the game out of the old coach.) Adopt these principles—better yet, live and breathe these principles—and you can build winning teams:

1. Play harder; play smarter; play together

2. Be willing to lose with the right people instead of winning with the wrong people

That's it. Everything else that goes into building cohesive, successful, hard-working and fully-functioning teams—and enjoying sports or professional success—flows from those two simple statements.

And by the way: The two principles must remain intact and are non-negotiable. They don't change based on different circumstances or under unusual conditions. In fact, when times get tough these two principles are even more important. It's fairly easy to sail when the wind is at your back, but great sailing crews can stay on course in almost every type of weather. As we'll talk about later, anyone can steer the ship when the water is calm.

Let's start with the first of my core philosophies: A team that plays harder, smarter, and together will almost always win, especially over the long term. (And if the team doesn't win, it's still the team I would choose to play for.) The key is to empower teammates or employees to do what they do best.

There are many ways to get the ball into the end zone. You can run, pass, score from the defensive side of the ball, or kick for points. So why not simply give players the ball and let them run?

In my company we don't care who gets the credit. When we do well, we all get the credit. As our salesperson you might, for instance, land the largest cup order in company history but if our manufacturing team can't meet the deadline...your individual achievement doesn't matter. Or flip it around: Our manufacturing team may be incredibly productive (and they are), but if our sales team can't win business, or if our shipping department delivers to the wrong warehouse...as an organization we still fail.

The entire team plays a critical role in *everything* we do. None of us succeeds alone.

Think in basketball terms. I often ask kids, "What are you willing to do to become a high school, college, or pro player? What are you *really* willing to do?" The correct answer to that question is, "I am willing to do whatever it takes."

Great players are almost always made—they are not born. Athletic talent only takes a person so far. (The basketball landscape is littered with gifted athletes who did not work hard to develop their games.) In business the same reasoning applies. Business is not a nine-to-five proposition; successful teams do whatever it takes for however long it takes. They make no excuses and they accept no excuses. Successful organizations do what it takes—and know they aren't in it alone. Every successful business embraces the fact that success is based on group, not individual, effort.

My second philosophy is just as critical. As a coach it didn't take me long to realize I would rather lose with the right people than win with the wrong people. If you have the wrong people you still may win some of the time, but when the going gets tough the wrong people will make poor decisions, will try to take the easy way out...that's why you must have the right people on your team. Every team will face adversity. It's only a matter of time.

Plus, in basketball it's just too long a season to spend hanging around with the wrong guys.

That's especially true in business, except the problem isn't that the season is so long—the problem is *life* is so short. I don't want to work with people who don't want to play harder, smarter, and together. The people who don't do things the right way eventually run out of road and go out of business.

Think of it this way: Some people will do whatever it takes to get an order. They will make unrealistic promises, agree to quality standards they know they cannot meet, or use sub-par materials or manufacturing techniques to offset the low prices they quote.

In our minds, those companies are taking *orders*. We get orders for cups, but what we really do is create *customers*. We develop repeat customers, loyal customers, and long-term programs because we do what we say we will do. We don't take orders; we create customers. There's a huge difference in taking orders and creating customers –the difference lies in consistent hard work performed by the right people in the right places.

The right people enjoy when others succeed. In high school I played on a basketball team that was good but certainly not great. We finished the regular season with a respectable record and late in the season we faced a very good team that had not lost a game, cruising to an unbeaten 16–0 record.

I'm proud to say we played them tough and were able to take their crowd out of the game, which in their gymnasium was never an easy feat. At the end of regulation the score was tied. The first overtime ended tied as well. Near the end of the second overtime period the score was still tied, and we actually had a chance to win.

During the game I was the leading scorer and had the most assists. During a time-out, with eight seconds to go in the second overtime, I told the team we could win. In fact, I told them I *knew* we could win. I took off down court when our center inbounded the ball to our other guard. All our other guard had to do was play quarterback, (which should have been easy because he was the quarterback on our football team), throw a long pass to me...and I make an easy layup. Game over. Harvey High School is 15–1.

But he didn't make the easy pass. Instead he took a three-quarter court shot that flew over the backboard. The game remained tied.

We lost the game in the third overtime.

When the final buzzer sounded their fans rushed the floor as my team struggled to make our way to the locker room. (I almost got trampled, and at least two different people punched me in the back while I was swimming against the tide of their celebrating fans.)

As we waited to board the bus I casually said to our other guard, "Tough game, huh?"

He nodded without looking at me.

At that point we had not had a chance to talk, so I asked, "Hey, at the end of the second overtime, did you see I was open on the inbounds play?"

He nodded again. Then he slowly turned and faced me.

"Yeah, I saw you were open," he said. "But I wasn't going to let you be the hero."

Great teams play harder, smarter, and together. He didn't want to be part of a great team—he was playing for his own team, for his own reasons, for his own motivations. At that moment I realized I would need to always pick my dance partners carefully. In high school you can't choose your teammates, but as a coach or a leader you absolutely can choose the people you work with.

We had the other team on the ropes. No one was within ten feet of me . . . but he didn't want me to be the hero.

That was more important to him than winning.

When times get tough, the wrong people will often let you down.

How do you pick the right people? It's hard. Finding employees who will fit into your system and who are committed to the organization's success is difficult. One key is to have one voice and one leader. Another is for every member of the team to know his or her role within the team. Manager manages; sales sells; manufacturers manufacture.

The best situations are when you have one team fighting one fight—and relying on each other. If you're in manufacturing, you shouldn't be worried about sales. If you're in manufacturing, you shouldn't worry about price levels. If you're in sales, you shouldn't worry about manufacturing costs. With the right people, in the right places, focused on doing their jobs to the best of their abilities and on working well with others on the team . . . with the right people you can, as a team and an organization, win.

But no matter how hard you try you may bring people in who turn out not to be the "right guys." What do you do when that happens? Make the decisions that have to be made—and make changes when necessary. Communicate what is not working. Give the employee a chance to meet expectations. Sometimes the problem is simply a lack of clear expectations, but most of the time you'll need to make a change and find someone who truly fits on the team you have built.

I often put this concept in basketball terms. If everyone on your team is a rebounder, you won't win. If you have five shooters on the floor, you won't win. (Plus you will have four problems since there is only one ball. With one ball, by definition four other players will be unhappy because they don't have the ball.)

For a leader, an employee who doesn't fit in and doesn't pull with the rest of the team creates a difficult work environment and presents quite a challenge. Do everything you can to make the situation work, but if that person can't work within the system, don't change the *system*. Change the *person*.

When you fire an employee you not only affect their employment status; you affect their family, their lifestyle, and their self-esteem. As a manager I have never "fired" anyone. Often what I do is bring the employee into my office, have them sit in my chair behind my desk, and talk them through some hypothetical issues and situations. Eventually they realize I'm not speaking hypothetically. I'm talking about them. Then I ask, "If you were in my position, sitting in that chair, what would you do?" Most say they would fire the person involved, so I take their resignation.

In sports, letting someone go is no easier. When you have to cut a player you cut a person who has worked incredibly hard, often for years. A lack of hard work and effort often isn't the problem; the problem is another player is bigger, stronger, faster, younger, more talented... and you have to make a change and go in a different direction. It's emotionally wrenching to watch a twenty-five year-old walk out the door after you just shattered his dreams.

Whenever a player—or an employee—walks out, you feel terrible.

If you don't feel terrible, I don't want to be a member of your team.

I don't sleep the night before I terminate an employee... or the night after. Making personnel changes is the hardest part of being a manager, a boss, or a leader. It's incredibly difficult. But you can make the process a little easier. The key is to avoid creating a confrontation. During training sessions I ask two new salespersons to face each other and put their hands in the air, palms touching the other person's. I tell one person to push; the other person automatically pushes back. Pushing back is human nature. When you discipline or terminate employees, many will "push" you—don't push back. They will only push back harder if you push back. Stay composed, stay professional, and treat those individuals with the dignity and respect they deserve.

And never, ever entertain a discussion or argument. If you aren't sure you're taking the right step in letting someone go, don't do it. When you're sure you are making the right decision there is no reason to argue.

Here's the bottom line: Empower your employees as long as they are worthy of being empowered—if they're not, make a change. Employees should earn empowerment based on hard work, reliability, and a demonstrated willingness to function within a team.

Again, the key is to make a change when things aren't working. Most people are afraid to make decisions that hurt people's feelings. Telling someone they are not performing well is never easy. Telling someone you must let them go because they are not performing to expectations is incredibly difficult. (If firing someone is easy for you, take a hard look in the mirror at the person you have become.)

As a leader you should never enjoy making changes, but making changes is your responsibility and one of your roles on the team.

If a team is held back or is under-performing due to one person, you must make a change. If someone isn't cutting it, you must release them. You can and should feel bad for that person, but you owe it to the rest of your team to make the change.

You will never enjoy firing people, but you will sleep better once you do . . . a couple of days later.

Remember, people have feelings but businesses don't. You can discipline or fire an employee professionally, with courtesy and respect. It's not easy—but sometimes it's necessary.

If an employee does not help your team work smarter, harder, and together . . . he or she has to go.

And while you would rather lose with the right people than win with the right people, in reality you'll find that you only win—long-term—with the right people.

Find them, empower them, and turn them loose.

That's how you build winning teams.

Four

Want to Make a Million Dollars? It's Only a Matter of Time

All of us work for two reasons and two reasons only: We work to make money and we work to have fun.

Of course it doesn't always work out that way. I know "poor" people who are incredibly happy, and I know millionaires who are absolutely miserable. The key, in work and in every other facet of life, is to create and maintain a balance. If you are making money but not having fun, you may need to make changes. If you're not making enough money but you are having a lot of fun, you also might need to make changes.

If you aren't making money and aren't having fun, you definitely need to make changes—starting today.

I often talk about money when I speak to corporate and professional groups. While every audience is different, and I tailor my presentation to the needs and interests of each group, I frequently start off talks by verbally sizing up the group.

I might start a speech by saying, "First impressions are really important. I already made a first impression on you, and you made a first impression on me. As a speaker I normally come across good groups, great groups, and fair groups. It's pretty rare to get an exceptional group. But based on my first impression, I think you are an exceptional group: In fact, I'm willing to bet that *everyone* here will make a million dollars."

The last sentence tends to get their attention. It works with corporate audiences and with kids at basketball camps. I make that claim with confidence because barring unusual circumstances, *everyone* in the group is likely to make a million dollars.

The only real variable is how long making a million dollars will take.

Time is the key variable. (Quick math: If you make $30,000 a year and you work for more than thirty-three years—say, between the ages of twenty-two and fifty-five—you'll make over a million dollars over the course of your working life.) The more you make per year, the less time it will take—but just about everyone will eventually make a million dollars.

That's why time and balance are completely intertwined. If you focus solely on making money and spend all your time in that pursuit, you may reach your million dollar goal more quickly...but you also may feel desperately unhappy along the way. On the other hand, if you focus primarily on happiness you may never make the money you desire. In life, in business, and in basketball, you cannot be all about one thing.

You must stay busy *and* balanced.

Take a step back. Making a million dollars is all about business. If you live a lifestyle similar to the average adult, you are awake for somewhere between fifteen and seventeen hours each day. Most adults work eight to ten hours a day, five days a week. Others work more hours a day, for up to seven days a week.

Regardless of how many hours you put in at your job, your "work day" is not done when the day is over. Successful people continue to develop themselves. They read. They attend seminars. They find ways to continue learning and developing skills. Continuing education is an integral component in a busy and balanced life and is, quite frankly, your duty as an employee and as a leader.

The same is true where college is concerned; most people go to college in order to get an education so they can later make money. But graduating from college is just the first step. The game isn't over. A college degree hopefully gives you a head start on your career, but a college degree is also a little like a driver's license. When you get a driver's license you are legally permitted to drive, but you aren't guaranteed you will drive a Mercedes. A college degree may help you qualify for certain opportunities, but a diploma in no way guarantees opportunities.

A college degree does not guarantee that you will make a million dollars—at least not quickly.

The key is to bring your best to whatever game you play. We don't expect basketball players to show up for training camp or for practice and not be in shape. You should never show up for your job or career out of shape, either.

Here's an analogy I use at basketball camps. I like to ask the kids, "Hey—how many of want to play in the NBA?"

They all raise their hands.

Then I ask, "How many of you are great video game players?"

Almost all of them keep their hands in the air.

"So tell me this," I say. "If you were in a car accident and needed an operation, would you want the surgeon who was great at video games or the surgeon who worked hard at his craft? Who would you go to—the one who goofs off whenever he can or the guy working hard to be the best?"

They usually get quiet at that point. Then I hit them with the big finish.

"If you want to be a great basketball player," I say, "go home and sell your video games. You can be a great basketball player or a great video game player . . . but you can't be both. Which is more important to you?"

Hopefully some of the kids listen and take the message to heart, because success is based on identifying clear goals and then doing everything possible to reach those goals.

Keep in mind it is twice as hard to get kids to accept the premise today than it was, say, twenty or thirty years ago. Times have definitely changed. What has not changed is the basic fact that if you pay the premium you reap the benefits.

That's how sports, business, and life work.

Each of us has to take responsibility for what we do—if it is to be, it's up to me.

Part of the problem facing kids today is there are a lot more avenues to travel than when I was a child. When I grew up we had three TV channels, no Internet, no computers, no cell phones, no video games...and in my case, no stereos. In fact, the first "gadget" I can remember was a hand calculator. I saw one but didn't own one since at the time calculators cost about $200. (Don't complain when you have to pay $4 to buy a new calculator.) But I can easily argue access to great technology does not necessarily improve a person's skills. I use a calculator, but I know how to do the underlying math, and I think that understanding of the principles of mathematics helps me work through issues and problems a little more easily.

Another societal change is that when I was young, at least in my neighborhood, most mothers didn't work. Moms stayed home, took care of the home and the kids...and kids like me left the house when the sun came up. The playground was like our home base during the day. Today most playgrounds are empty—unless kids are there with their parents. Children don't go to the playground to play ball—they are at home letting technology entertain them.

Don't get me wrong. I don't believe technological advances are bad or harmful in and of themselves. What I do believe is that evolving technologies and family lifestyles have changed how kids grow up, how they approach sports, and in some ways how they approach life in general. Take me: I grew up in a post-war environment. I was part of a culture where families moved from the cities to the suburbs, employment was stable, and most people were relatively unpretentious.

Today, sadly, much of that is no longer the case. I often see situations where parents buy their children things in an effort to offset or replace the fact that neither parent is home much of the time. Spending is a way for parents to ease a little of the guilt or regret they feel—but in reality spending doesn't help the parent or the child.

When I was in school, if I got in trouble I didn't want to go home—I knew the reception I would receive. Today when behavioral issues pop up many parents go to the principal not to find out what happened and how to correct the situation, but instead to back their kids.

Instead of learning to be good citizens and to fit in, many kids want to make their own "statements"—and their parents support them.

Times have also changed where coaching is concerned. I respected my coaches, but I was also scared of my coaches. Each of my coaches was the *boss*. Inside I may not have agreed with certain decisions, but I didn't say so out loud—that wasn't my place. (And a lot of the time what I thought was wrong, although I didn't realize it at the time.)

In my day the coach was in charge. Today the kids think they run the teams. (And in many cases they do.) With private jets flying AAU teams to summer tournaments, who can blame kids for thinking they are in charge?

In my opinion we won't see another Michael Jordan. I'm not saying another player with his level of talent won't come along—that could very well happen. But what will never happen is a situation where a "Michael Jordan" gets cut from his high school team and later achieves incredible success. Michael was cut from a team, went home, worked hard, did what he needed to do to make the team the next year...and the rest is basketball history. The average kid today is not likely to dig deep to overcome a short-term failure and do whatever it takes to succeed. Kids won't reach down to do what they have to do because, quite frankly, they don't feel they need to. When times get tough they will simply drift away...and a potential Michael Jordan will be lost forever.

What other factors have led to a major shift from a basketball (and sports in general) point of view? Here's one causal factor: ESPN. I have absolutely nothing against ESPN, but one outcome of featuring "highlights" is kids tend to only see dunks, long three-pointers, and hot dog plays. Highlights are certainly part of the game, but highlights only make up a small portion of any game. Yet if you are a kid and you just watched Sports Center, what will you be likely to do when you pick up a ball? Will you work on fundamentals like dribbling, passing, layups, and jump shots?

Or will you start tossing up threes and lowering the rim so you can practice dunks?

A trend towards organization has also affected most sports. When I was young we played on organized teams, but organized activities only made up a small percentage of the time we actually spent playing a sport. Take baseball, for example: My youth league teams typically practiced a couple of hours a week, and our weekly games lasted a couple of hours. Add it up and I spent about four hours total each *week* playing organized baseball . . . but in the summertime I played six or eight hours each *day* on the playground.

Organized sports only take kids so far. Coaches, especially youth coaches, can only do so much to develop player skills. Time in the backyard, on the playground, in the gym, and on the field is absolutely vital.

Today, 80% of all kids stop playing organized sports after the age of twelve. Kids stop playing when they no longer have fun. Some have less fun and lose interest because of lack of playing time, others due to the quality of youth coaching, and still others due to pressure from parents. Whatever the reason, it's incredibly sad. (Oddly enough the fastest-growing activity for kids is extreme sports; there are no coaches, no organizations, and no pressure . . . just friends encouraging each other and applauding each other's accomplishments.)

Think about it: How many pickup baseball games have you seen lately? How many pickup football games have you seen lately? How many times have you driven by a field and seen six or eight kids playing a game of soccer—without parents, officials, or coaches?

I'm guessing very few—if any.

Increased athletic specialization is also a factor. As recently as ten to twenty years ago, most high school athletes played two or three sports. Now many specialize. They lift weights and work out in the offseason instead of playing another sport. I loved basketball, but in high school I ran on an undefeated cross country team and ran track as well. It never occurred to me to specialize, and after all why would I want to? Playing other sports was too much fun. I wish I could have played baseball as well; it was my best sport. But since baseball and track fell in the same season, I chose to run track.

I can't deny specialization is probably with us to stay, and most kids will need to adapt to the situation. When parents ask, I tell them to let their kids have fun and play as many different sports as they want as they grow up. In ninth grade a child may be forced to choose one particular sport, but if that becomes necessary the child should choose the sport, not the parent. You may want your child to earn a basketball scholarship, but statistically speaking the odds of that happening are fairly slim. There are certainly no guarantees. What you can guarantee is that a child who plays a high school sport will feel a real sense of pride and will have a lot of fun being part of a team.

So why shouldn't kids play the sport or sports they love best?

Speaking of scholarships, I cannot count how many parents have asked me to help their children get scholarships. I can't help, necessarily, but I can give advice. Here's what I say.

Say I'm a college coach. I work hard to scout players. I go to AAU tournaments, to basketball camps, to high
school games...I work incredibly hard to know the players.
But I can't know everyone, so a player who makes the effort
to contact me will have a slightly greater chance of getting
noticed. As a result, some kids send tapes and stats; others
pay services to pull together video clips and create packages
to send to coaches.

But that's me—some coaches don't look at player sub-
missions. Many schools, especially larger programs, have
already identified the athletes they are interested in. If you
have not earned a spot on their radar screens, contacting
the coach won't help. Smaller Division I schools, Division
II schools, and junior colleges are more likely to take a look
at some of the players who contact them.

I also remind parents that every coach tries to create
balance on his or her team. Your son might be the best
player on his team, in his conference, or even in his state, but
think of it this way: If your son is an outstanding rebounder
and a team already has three solid power forwards who can
rebound like a young, svelte Charles Barkley...there might
not be a place for your son in that particular program.
Coaches strive to create balance and fill needs, and not every
star player meets the needs of a particular team.

Then I ask parents about motivation. Many parents
want their kids to earn scholarships, and that's fine...but
what is most important is that the *child* wants to be an
outstanding *player*. My son Brendan played Division I
basketball. Playing college basketball was his dream, not

mine. He wasn't a great player but he wanted to play in college. He put in the work, hit the weights, and did what great players do. He earned his spot on the team and on the floor. He worked hard because he loved the game, not because he wanted to earn a scholarship. A scholarship would have been a by-product of his efforts and not the ultimate goal.

But his road wasn't easy, and is a nice reminder of the fact that often you cannot pick the situation you find yourself in—but you still have to do your best with the cards you are dealt. When Brendan was in junior high he was good basketball player. He was what basketball people affectionately call a gym rat—he spent hours and hours in the gym working on his game. (If you're not familiar with the term, don't assume "gym rat" is a negative term—Larry Bird was considered a gym rat.) He also played on an AAU travel team that I coached. He was a solid but not a spectacular player.

His high school team was, well, not very good. In fact, during some quarters of games they were unable to score any points at all. Brendan rarely played, even though (and I'm speaking objectively) he certainly was good enough to play. He often came home discouraged, so I kept telling him to keep his mouth shut, play hard, and always do his best.

One game he was called off the bench early in the first quarter. His assignment was to guard the best player on the other team. Defense is all about attitude, and Brendan has a never-say-die attitude; at halftime he had shut down the other player while scoring eighteen points himself. Sadly, the coach did not play Brendan in the second half, and the next few games he didn't play at all.

But he still wanted to play college basketball. Since he had almost no high school experience, larger schools showed no interest. So he visited local Division III schools and convinced the coach at Avila University to let him try out for the team. He enrolled, made the team, and enjoyed solid freshman and sophomore seasons.

At Christmas he came home and said, "Dad, I've been thinking. I would like to be a coach someday. In fact I would like to be a Division I coach." As an old coach I know how the system works, and I told him he would need to play for a Division I program in order to have a good shot at someday earning a coaching job at a Division I school. (You may think that sounds unfair, but that is how it tends to work.)

I could tell he was serious, so I called Bob Huggins, then the head coach at the University of Cincinnati, at his home on New Year's Eve day. (Today Bob is the head coach at West Virginia University.) I said, "Bob, you know my son. He's a good kid, a good student, and a good team player. He'll never win a game for you but he'll never lose a game for you either...and he'll give you everything he has in games and in practice."

Bob said, "I have an open slot, but there's one catch— he has to be enrolled at Cincinnati in three days in order to be eligible."

So on New Year's Eve I asked my son, "How would you like to go to Cincinnati?"

He immediately said yes.

So we loaded up the car, drove to Cincinnati, and he spent a year on the team. In fact, Bob liked him so much Brendan became the son Bob never had.

But there was one problem: Brendan was a good basketball player, but he was not quick enough to guard his position at that level. ("Guarding your position" is an old basketball philosophy: You may have certain skills, but if you can't guard the opponent who plays your position, you won't make it.) So Bob offered him a position as a student assistant. Later when Bob took the head coaching job at Kansas State, Brendan followed him there as a graduate assistant, earning a Master's degree in the process.

Today Brendan is a junior college coach in Florida, working hard and paying his dues to make it to the Division I level.

Brendan could have become discouraged in high school and walked away from the sport and from his dreams. Instead he dealt with adversity, kept working hard, found a way to play in college, played for a nationally-ranked Division I program as a walk-on, became a student assistant, became a graduate assistant...and today is still following his dream.

At any point along the way he could have quit, but he didn't.

As you can guess, I'm very proud of him—as I am of both of our kids.

Today Brendan will tell you that when you are coaching or leading, players and employees learn from you in two different ways. They learn *what* to do and what *not* to do.

In high school he learned the wrong way to treat people. In college he learned the right way to treat people.

If you love the game and want to be the best, you will work hard. If you love your job and want to succeed, you'll work hard and you won't let adversity or roadblocks set you back.

Success is a by-product of hard work and effort. There is no short cut to success and enjoying what you do. You can make your million dollars—and you can enjoy your work and your life.

The key is balance—and balance starts with dreaming your own dreams, setting your own goals, and enjoying what you do along the way.

Five

My Parents

Want to know how to creatively solve complex, multi-layered problems? Ask my parents.

My father was an executive for a company called White Consolidated Industries, Inc. He was the President of a subsidiary of White Consolidated called Columbus Products. Columbus Products made refrigerators. White Consolidated Industries purchased Frigidaire, and my dad took care of the takeover and retired soon after the transition, having served the company for over thirty-five years.

Clearly he was a busy guy.

He was also busy at home. And with six kids in the family, my parents realized it was very likely four of us would be in college at the same time. He wanted us all to go to college.

My dad was big on education. He received his undergraduate and Master's degrees from the University of Pittsburgh.

Big on education or not, college is expensive. College for six kids is very expensive.

So my father opened a soft-serve ice cream store. We called it Foley's Karnival Cream.

Having "Foley's" in the name was appropriate because it truly was a family business. How "family" was the business? From the ages of twelve to seventeen, I worked in the store. During those years, so did my brothers and sisters. The store was open from spring through fall. My job was to get to the store by 10 a.m., get things ready, open the store for business at 11 a.m., and work until 4 p.m. I waited on customers, made ice cream, cleaned the equipment and the floors and the windows...I did it all.

We all did. My brother Kevin worked afternoons, my two sisters, Ellen and Debbie, worked evenings. My oldest brother Jim, who's "day job" was buyer of women's shoes for May Company Department Stores, worked weekends along with the rest of us. Open from 11 a.m. to 11 p.m., seven days a week, from April 15th through November 1st, Foley's Karnival Cream was a total family enterprise that we operated for seven years.

The business taught us all a lot. We learned how to deal with customers, make a quality product, build a clientele, handle money, deal with problems...we even learned a little about accounting.

None of us got rich, even though the store was always busy. Stopping by the store for ice cream was a community activity. Some evenings customers would line up twenty-deep in lines stretching all the way to the street; local youth teams would stop by after games. Getting rich wasn't the point.

My father started the business as a type of college fund; his goal was to put aside enough money to pay for all of us to go to college. I didn't get rich. My brothers and sisters didn't get rich. I earned the princely sum of $10 per week. I had no idea what my wages worked out to in terms of an hourly rate, and I didn't care.

Every Sunday night we held a family business meeting. We sat down at the kitchen table to go over the previous week's financial results. We also received our $10 wages, which of course was gratifying, but over time I started to feel a greater sense of pride in the money we were able to put in our college fund every week. Even when I was twelve years old I realized how much fun it is to be part of something larger than myself.

I started to understand how much fun it could be to be part of lots of different types of teams—in this case a business team.

The Sunday night business meetings were my father's main contribution to the business—in addition to his executive position he was also the mayor of our town, so he really didn't have time to work in the store. He never sold an ice cream cone, but on Sunday mornings he did hose down the parking lot while he talked to some of his buddies (proving that in the right situations you really can talk and work at the same time.) His contribution was instead much greater and longer-lasting: He taught us to think ahead, to develop plans, to execute those plans…he taught us how to deal with customers, to take responsibility…and most importantly he taught us how to put in the work necessary to achieve our goals.

We all wanted to go to college—he showed us how to earn that right and that privilege. (As it turns out we earned the right through other means as well. We all went to college, and my brother and I earned athletic scholarships while my sisters earned education scholarships.)

I also learned how to manage my time. I woke up early each day so I could shoot free throws and still make it to the store by 10 a.m. On weekdays I would ride my bike the 1.5 miles to the store. On Sundays I would run to the store and back. Once I got off work at 4 p.m. I would rush home, grab a quick snack, and head to the local park. Kids from five or six communities showed up and we played ball every night from around 5.30 until the lights were turned out at 10 p.m. I would then go straight to bed, because for several years I also had two paper routes I took care of in the morning.

I was busy, but I loved it.

Oh—speaking of busy, I also sold seeds door to door when I was younger because I wanted to buy a new Rawlings Mickey Mantle glove. I also sold enough seeds to earn a bugle; I bet my father wished he simply paid for the glove in order to save the family and neighbors from the sound of my enthusiastic but less than accomplished bugle playing.

And during a junior high candy sale, I sold more candy than any other student just so I could get first choice of the prizes. One of the prizes was a leather gym bag—my coach had a bag just like it, and I really wanted that bag. So I did what it took to earn it.

My brothers and sisters approached life the same way: If we saw an opportunity, we took it. We did whatever it took to reach our goals.

Our father taught—no, let me rephrase that—our father *showed* us how to earn opportunities. His example is a lesson I have never forgotten, and one my wife and I tried hard to pass on to our children.

So we learned a lot from running the family business, but in some ways I think we learned more from the time we spent at our dining room table. In the winter, every night at 6 p.m. (sharp!) we ate dinner as a family. As I mentioned earlier my father loved to turn dinner into an informal quiz session. He asked questions about history, math, business...but he also asked a lot of fun questions.

For example, he might say, "A bus carrying forty people pulls up. Ten get on and five get off; at the next stop eight people get off and three get on; multiply by two, minus ten; at the next stop fifteen get off, nine get on; at the next stop..." While he spoke all of us would feverishly do the mental math, trying to keep up with the number of passengers still on the bus.

When he was done he would say, "Okay. Now, how many stops did the bus make?" Of course we wouldn't know—we had been too busy tracking the number of passengers.

My dad was an original. At his funeral I was asked to speak. I didn't prepare. Off the cuff, I said, "My father liked to look at things differently. He was the kind of guy who would say during a rain storm, 'I hope the rain keeps up...because if it keeps up it won't come down.'" I talked about how even though he was an executive and the mayor of our town he always made time for his family. He never missed dinner, never missed any games, and never missed school events. He came home from work at 5.30, we ate as a family at 6:00, and by 7:00 he would be in his office at city hall. Saturday mornings he spent at city hall as well.

My father was involved in city politics for eighteen years, not because he wanted power or craved attention but because he felt it was his duty to give back to his community. Born in Pittsburgh, he played quarterback at Pitt and later played baseball in the St. Louis Browns organization. When he returned from World War II, he and my mother moved into a small home in the suburbs of Cleveland and he quickly realized there were no youth sports or recreation programs available for area children. So instead of complaining or ignoring the problem, he started the first youth organizations in the area. He thought youth activities were important. He wasn't into *politics*. He was into *kids* and *recreation*. Politics was not his vocation, it was his avocation.

People in the community recognized his efforts and convinced him to run for city council. Later he ran for mayor, and in subsequent mayoral elections often ran unopposed. He loved serving the community but as his business obligations increased and his family grew he finally decided something had to give—and family was the last thing that would "give." So at the end of his last term he gave up his political life.

I think my mom missed community activities more than my dad, but in true Foley spirit she put her efforts where her heart was. She served as the foundation of our family, but she did a lot more than just raise her children. For example, in Ohio at that time there were no programs or facilities for people who were mentally retarded. Mentally handicapped children were often placed in state institutions. The situation was heartbreaking, so my mother became chairman of the county mental retardation board. (Not only did she become chairman—I think she created the organization itself.)

Instead of placing people in institutions, her vision was to create a workshop-like setting for people to attend during the day and return to their homes at night. While that approach sounds straightforward—and in fact is the model most communities follow today—at the time it was a revolutionary concept and went completely against mainstream thinking. (Not to mention against the state's position on "dealing with" people who were mentally retarded.) So my mother founded a facility called Deep Wood Retardation Center. Her efforts were so unpopular that for a time people in the community picketed our home in protest. Again, today many similar centers exist around the country, but at the time it was an incredibly unpopular move.

The tide of public opinion grew strong enough local news crews filmed the protests. So here I was at twelve watching people carrying signs, chanting chants, and picketing our house. I was afraid to go outside...but I also learned, at a young age, how the unpopular thing to do might also be the *right* thing to do. My mother liked to say,

"Sometimes you will know the right thing to do because it will be the hardest thing to do."

My mother felt she was doing the right thing—and she was. So she kept her head down, kept working, overcame obstacles, and made a real difference in peoples' lives. She explained to me why what she was doing was important, and helped me understand how people less fortunate than us really needed our help.

I learned a lot from my parents, but in particular my father taught me to decide what I wanted, to develop a plan to get me there, and to do whatever it took to reach my goals. My mother taught me, by words and by example, to forge ahead to do what I feel is right, regardless of what other people might think or how unpopular my stance might be.

In short, my parents led by words and by deeds. My parents not only made decisions but helped us understand the reasoning behind those decisions. They created—and shared—goals for us as a family and as individuals. They helped us understand the right, and the wrong, way to reach our goals and follow our dreams.

My parents raised us the right way.

Along the way they taught us about business and about running a business. The lessons I learned have continued to serve me well to this day.

Thanks, mom and dad. I owe you more than I can ever repay...but hopefully I have repaid some of that debt by raising our children using the example you set for my brothers and sisters and I.

Six

Running an Organization: Basketball or Business

I love practice.

As a player and as a coach, I love basketball practice. Games are fun, sure, but games are relatively infrequent events. Practice is a nearly every day event. Practice is when, as a player, you develop skills, improve teamwork, try out new things... it's hard to learn and develop during a game. Practice is where you grow as an athlete and as a person.

Most kids go to practice and do what the coach says. But, "doing what the coach says" can vary greatly from coach to coach. When I was in high school and even when I was in college my coaches didn't follow a practice plan. I think they knew, in their heads, what they wanted to do that day, but they didn't write it down and they certainly didn't communicate the plan to their players. As players we showed up and did what we were told.

At the pro level we followed detailed practice plans and the difference in results was dramatic. My first professional head coach, Kevin Pritchard (until recently the General Manager of the Portland Trailblazers), developed extensive practice plans. He learned how from some of his earlier coaches, Larry Brown, today the coach of the Charlotte Bobcats, and from Roy Williams, currently head coach at the University of North Carolina...who learned from Dean Smith...who learned from Phog Allen...who learned from Dr. Naismith.

That is one great coaching tree.

Following practice plans can create a drastic improvement in team planning, execution, and philosophy. All teams—whether basketball or business—play like they practice. There is no magic light switch that can be turned on and off. Sloppy practices lead to sloppy games. A lack of discipline in practice leads to a lack of discipline during games. Players who are not required to focus during practice can hardly be expected to maintain focus when faced with a hostile crowd at the end of a close game.

It's just not possible.

Organization starts at the top. I'm huge on organization. I'm proud of the attention to detail and level of organization we bring to the table at Dynamic Drinkware. I'm proud I'm a product of basketball people like Kevin

Pritchard Larry Brown and Roy Williams. I wish other people were able to enjoy the opportunities I have been given to learn from the best.

Where did I learn from the best? I learned from them at practice.

Here's how the best basketball practices are run. I'll use my coaching philosophies as an example. (You'll notice running a basketball practice is a lot like running a business.)

Every day we created and printed a practice plan. Each plan was thorough and detailed and every activity and drill was broken down into discrete time periods. To stay on track we ran the game clock, shifting from drill to drill at specific, pre-determined intervals.

But the practice plan wasn't just a tool for coaches to use.

To get players to buy into the practice plan, we posted copies in the locker room and taped copies to each goal post. If practice was scheduled to officially start at 3 p.m., players were expected to be on the floor no less than twenty minutes early, warming up and getting ready so we could start on time. Players came in, reviewed the practice plan, and mentally prepared for what we expected to accomplish that day.

Players also had homework. Every practice plan included a specific focus. At the end of each day's practice we discussed what the focus would be for the next practice. At 3 o'clock we blew the whistle, gathered the players, and asked random players to share the focus for that day's practice. Usually the focus was fairly simple: Make the extra pass, block out, hit outlet passes, set good hard picks... but if the player called on was unable to recall the focus for the day, every player had to run suicides as a "punishment."

Why did *every* player have to run? Our goal was to promote individual performance by creating team repercussions for a lack of effort, preparation, or execution. Most people don't want to be a weak link. Most people try harder when they don't want to let down their peers. (Believe me: The last thing a player wants to do is be responsible for making his teammates run suicides.)

At the beginning of practice we also asked one player to come up with a "thought for the day" for the next day. The thought of the day could be sports-related, family-related, or business-related... it didn't matter as long as the thought of the day was something the team could buy into. Most thoughts of the day were fairly simple. (At least one player bought a book of famous quotations so he would always be ready if called on. That was fine with me. He wasn't cheating; he was taking steps to ensure he would always be prepared.)

I feel developing, sharing, and following a practice plan was important, and I'm in good company: The late John Wooden, arguably the most successful college basketball coach in history—and without argument the most beloved—ran his practices from sets of note cards that specified the drill, the time period, the goal of the drill... he knew exactly what he wanted to accomplish during every single minute of every practice. Ten national championships later, it's hard to argue with his approach.

If you're a coach and you don't follow a practice plan, you should. Your team will be better organized, better prepared, and better able to play as a team.

The same is true in business. Every member of every team is important. Every person needs to know what goals are important to the business and how he or she contributes to reaching those goals. Your business should run by a plan that helps employees understand their roles and their goals. For example, some sales teams meet every day. Some production teams meet every day. How often teams meet isn't important—what is important is the types of discussions take place and the types of decisions that are made during the meeting. The *meeting* itself isn't important; the *outcomes* of the meeting are important.

Your meetings should be planned in a way to ensure the outcomes you desire. If you want to make a decision about an important issue, plan the meeting so a decision can be made. If you want to change a procedure, plan the meeting so you can share the procedure, answer questions, and ensure understanding and buy-in.

If you don't know what you want to accomplish and how you will accomplish it...don't have the meeting. If you aren't ready, you can hardly expect your employees to be ready.

Focus is the key. Focus starts, in my opinion, with being on time. When I worked for Purolator we locked the meeting room door when a meeting started. If a meeting was scheduled for 8 a.m., at 8 a.m. the door to the room was locked. Ten minutes after the meeting started we unlocked the door to let any stragglers in. Not only did latecomers have to endure the shame of being late, but in order to enter the room they faced an additional punishment: The group would make latecomers sing, or dance...whatever we decided the punishment for arriving late should be.

The point of locking the door was not to humiliate people but simply to reinforce the importance of being on time. (And have a little fun in the process.)

It worked. If you know you will be locked out of a meeting if you show up late...and you will have to sing to be allowed to join the group...believe me, you will show up on time.

And you will recognize, without having to be told, the importance of the meeting. Meetings are like practices: In many organizations, meetings are where results are shared, plans are made, goals are set—without great "practices" your team cannot play great "games."

By the way; we don't lock the door to meetings at Dynamic Drinkware. We don't have to—everyone shows up on time, ready to roll.

Meetings are also a great way to practice daily themes. Some organizations meet daily, and their meetings have daily themes. Salespeople talk about sales. Production people talk about production. Every meeting should have a daily theme, and the more you reinforce your daily themes, the more your team will follow those themes. The result is a more productive and successful team.

You'll be surprised what themes can, over time, take hold in an organization. A Vice President of Sales who works for one of our largest customers sends out a thought of the day by email. He sends the email to everyone on his team, plus to other people outside the organization (like me.) Some thoughts of the day he makes up. Others he gets from books or magazines. At first people thought the emails were, to be honest, a little silly and even a waste of time. But then he missed a few days, and many of the people on his email list were disappointed not to receive a thought of the day. His emails had become a theme in their daily work life—a theme they looked forward to.

Over time the practice became ingrained and important.

History repeats itself.

What history do you want to repeat? Identify key themes, and reinforce the history you want to build in your meetings.

Keep in mind you don't have to reinvent the wheel. All you have to do is use what works. Look around; there are plenty of examples you can follow. For example, as a coach I didn't always study game tapes to find ways to attack other teams' weaknesses; I often looked for schemes or strategies I could borrow that my team could benefit from.

By the way, I'm often asked, so here's a quick aside about game video. Video study is very important in a sport like football, where games are only played once a week and twenty-two players are on the field at one time. As a coach it is easy to miss a lot from the sidelines; too much is going on. Video is priceless. On the other hand, video study is important but certainly less critical in sports like basketball and baseball. As a coach in those sports you watch your team play, in person, almost every day; it's impossible to spend time in the video room breaking down every game. That's why basketball coaches use video to confirm overall impressions, to spot weaknesses in other teams, and to "steal" ideas that can be applied to their own teams.

As we like to say, "The eye in the sky doesn't lie." Video shows you when a player works harder on offense than on defense. You can see if picks are solidly set. You can identify when a player goes under a screen instead of on top of the screen. You can see when players are working hard, and when they take plays off. Video is a little like a productivity report since it quantities and records results.

But video can also be over-used. As a coach I didn't spend hours reviewing game tapes. Players don't need to spend hours reviewing game tapes either. Spending more than twenty to thirty minutes showing game tape to players in any one session can be counter-productive. So I looked for little things. Most coaches try to pick out moments they can use to show players how they could approach specific situations differently. Video is great for creating discrete teachable moments, but if misused or over-used can become a visual hammer that can pound the confidence out of your players. Players want to *play*—they don't want to watch video after painful video showing their mistakes.

The same thing is true in business, especially where mistakes are concerned. A few years ago a customer gave us a very large order. We ran the job, and three weeks later our customer service rep accidentally re-entered the order. So we automatically re-ran the order, even though the customer didn't actually order more cups. Oops. (Okay, *big* oops.)

What did we do? One, we recognized the customer service rep didn't make the mistake on purpose. That individual simply made a mistake. Some organizations would have fired the employee. We saw the situation not just as an unfortunate and expensive mistake but also a mistake we could benefit from in the long run. We talked about what happened, identified the flaw in our current system, and put procedures in place to ensure the same type of mistake would not be made in the future.

As a leader, you cannot control or prevent human error. What you can do is keep a mistake from occurring a second time. We tell all of our employees: "Make all the mistakes you want...just don't duplicate them." Eventually, over time, people run out of mistakes to make. (Sometimes I think the best employees are the ones who made a lot of mistakes early on; making mistakes is probably one of the most valuable forms of training.)

When you establish a business culture that learns from mistakes, you develop great employees.

The same coaching and team attitude also develops better players. In basketball, one of the worst mistakes a player can make is committing a turnover leading to a score by the other team. No player wants to turn the ball over, but it happens multiple times every game. Turnovers are simply a part of basketball because no player is perfect. Yet committing a turnover is not the worst thing a player can do; the worst thing a player can do is to sulk or pout afterwards and therefore compound the problem. Dwelling on an error is like making a second mistake. Great athletes and great employees have short memories. Turnovers and mistakes happen; when they do, go on to the next play. A great golfer doesn't look back and dwell on the fact he missed a critical putt. He accepts it, tries to learn from it, puts it away... and forgets about it.

If you make a great play, wonderful—now forget it. If you make a bad play, that's too bad—now forget it. Either way you still have to make the next play. You always have to make the next play. If you make a big sale, don't go celebrate—make another sale. Don't walk away. Don't stop until the numbers tell you to stop.

It is your job as a leader to foster that kind of team environment. Anyone can steer the ship when the waters are calm. Great leaders steer when the waves are high, the seas are choppy, and navigation seems impossible. Great teams can help steer the ship when they practice like they want to play. You cannot expect your team to perform when times are tough unless you have taught them how to perform. Running a business and coaching a team is stressful. Practice, and reinforcing common themes, is designed to ensure your teams are ready to handle choppy seas.

Think of it this way: If you want to take the stress and uncertainty out of your business life, all you need to do is find a job where you receive a shirt with your name on it. Then the most difficult thing you'll probably do is ask people if they want fries with their order.

In a business environment, every action and every decision impacts the next move you make. If you manage reactively, you still have the same level of stress—or greater—but you'll have a lot bigger problems and issues to overcome. Be proactive and your job will still be stressful, but you can manage and control that stress and the outcomes of your decisions.

And most importantly, trust your experience and your instincts. I use numbers to judge performance where possible; liars can figure but figures can't lie. But I also focus on intangibles.

For example, if an employee is at his desk but not answering his phone, something is wrong. If the phone rings and you're afraid to pick it up, you must have done something wrong. There must be a problem you hope to avoid. Maybe you didn't meet a scheduled delivery. Maybe you messed up an order. Maybe you didn't follow up and the customer is mad. I may not know what the exact problem is—but if you are not answering the phone, I do know there's a problem.

The same thing holds true in meetings. If an employee "forgot" to bring last week's results, or launches into a long-winded explanation of why he did not meet a particular goal, I know there's something wrong. Good employees are willing to share good news and bad news. Good employees accept responsibility when things don't go well, and instead of focusing on why they did not achieve their goals spend time sharing exactly how they plan to overcome the obstacles they face. As a player and as an employee, you won't always win—but you should always try to win and plan to win.

Failing to prepare is preparing to fail.

Don't tell me why you lost; tell me how you will win.

That way I can help you win. The best part about winning and losing is that both are temporary. Win or lose, the sun comes up tomorrow, and you get to start the process all over again, each and every day.

The most important ingredient in building winning teams is for people to understand that employees do not work for the boss. Bosses work for employees. Our employees do not work for *me*—I work for *them*. I'm a tool. Tell me what you need. Managers don't "do." Managers set direction, establish goals, and oversee. Managers make sure all the tools are in place and all the details are taken care of. Employees do; managers manage. Your job as a leader and manager, each and every day, is to work for your employees.

It's not the other way around—not if you want to build winning teams.

Seven

Setting Goals—and Sharing Goals

As they walked in the door for the first time, I asked each player a simple question.

"What is your ring size?"

In professional sports, champions get rings. The tradition extends to many college sports as well. Players who win Super Bowls get rings. Players who win World Series get rings. NBA champions receive rings commemorating their achievement. Players on each year's NCAA men's and women's basketball teams receive rings.

In 2010 the New Orleans Saints won the Super Bowl. Under the terms of the collective bargaining agreements, players received an $83,000 bonus for winning the game. $83,000 is a lot of money, even to a professional athlete, but I'm guessing if you ask each player whether the money or the ring means more to them . . . to a person they will choose the ring.

Money is important, sure. But the ring is a symbol of achievement that lasts forever, long after the money is gone. A Super Bowl ring is a tangible symbol of a goal achieved.

So at the start of the season I asked my players for their ring size. Only champions receive rings. By asking for their ring size I let my players know everything they needed to know about my goals: I wanted to win.

In my opinion, setting goals is not just important. Sharing goals makes all the difference.

I asked for ring sizes for a secondary reason as well. At the time I was coaching in the American Basketball Association, a men's professional basketball league. The ABA is a developmental league for players hoping to move to the next level—the NBA. The ABA serves a similar function to minor league baseball, but unlike the minor league system in baseball, ABA teams are not affiliated with specific NBA teams. (For example, in major league baseball the Iowa Cubs are the AAA affiliate of the Chicago Cubs. Players on the Iowa team are under contract to the Cubs organization, and move up and down within that organization unless they are traded or released.) Players in the ABA are free agents in the truest sense of the term—they can be signed by any NBA team at any time.

Many of the players on our team had at one time played under NBA contracts. Some had played in the NBA for a year, two years . . . a few for as many as fourteen years. Those players were incredibly hungry to make it back to the NBA.

Shoot, who am I kidding? Every player on our team and in the league was incredibly hungry to make it to the NBA. Every player wanted to make it to the next level so they could compete against the best.

But every player also wanted to make it to the next level for economic reasons.

It's easy to assume all NBA players are wealthy. Since Kobe Bryant made over $24 million in salary alone last year, it's an easy assumption to make. Yet the typical player makes a lot less. The minimum salary for a first-year player is a little over $470,000 per year; nothing to sneeze at but only a small fraction of what a player like Kobe earns. Each year the minimum salary rises, and by year five the minimum salary a player can be paid is a little over $1 million.

$1 million is a lot of money, but consider this: The average length of an NBA career is 4.8 seasons. And like any average, that figure is somewhat misleading: For every player like Jason Kidd, who just completed his 16th season, countless players only stay in the league for a year or two. Averages are always skewed by extremes, and that's especially true where the NBA is concerned. A huge percentage of players don't make it to their third year (which is a shame since after three years NBA players qualify for a retirement pension. Under the current pension plan, a player who is vested for the three-year minimum will at age 62 receive an annual benefit of $56,988.)

In short, the pay in the NBA is obviously excellent, and there is also a significant long-term financial incentive to play in the league for at least three seasons. Aside from achieving their dream of playing at the highest level, that's why every player in a developmental league like the ABA wants to make it to—or back to—the NBA.

So how do you make it back to the NBA?

Win. Making it back is all about winning.

You might assume the average player in a development league focuses solely on individual statistics, and that is certainly true to in some instances and to some degree. Players hoping for a shot need to stand out from the crowd. Statistics certainly help them stand out.

But NBA coaches are incredibly smart. They know almost any player can rack up huge personal statistics as long as he is willing to sacrifice team play for individual "glory." If you are a good player increasing your points per game average is relatively easy: The more you shoot, the more you score, the more your stats go up. Sounds easy, right?

NBA coaches checking out players in a developmental league are not looking for the next superstar. They draft their superstars. They trade for their superstars. They sign superstars as free agents. Superstars are already playing in the league. When coaches comb the developmental leagues for players, they look for "team" guys: Players who can fill a specific role, who will work hard in practice, who will challenge the starters and help them become better players...NBA coaches look for players who bring qualities that will help the team win.

That's why NBA coaches look for winners. If you can't win at a lower level you won't win at a higher level. It's that simple. (The premise is similar to working in a corporate setting: If you can't excel in a lower-level position, why should you be promoted to a higher-level position?) Players in our league were there for one reason and one reason only: They wanted to show NBA coaches what they could do. They wanted to win. They wanted to excel.

But to show what they could do, they wanted—no, they *needed*—to play.

As the coach, I held the keys to the playing car. I decided who played and who did not play. That's why I asked each player for his ring size: I wanted each one to know my focus was on winning. If you helped us win, you would play. Players figured out pretty quickly that working towards team goals was important. If they didn't figure it out, they didn't play. When goals are clear, when expectations are clear, and when repercussions for failing to meet expectations are clear... most people figure out what to do and what not to do fairly fast.

If they don't figure it out, it's your job to make a change.

I'm proud to say nine of our players were signed by NBA teams during one season alone. We knew guys would go. We hoped guys would go. I wanted to see them succeed. Even though losing our best players definitely impacted our chances of winning, I didn't really mind seeing them move up. I was proud to play a part in helping players achieve their dreams.

We dealt with continuous change. That was the nature of the beast. Great people move up. Great people move out. In sports and in business cream eventually rises to the top.

I share my ABA experience for one main reason: Discussing my experiences as an ABA coach is the perfect way to illustrate how individual goals and team goals can mesh. Sometimes, in some settings, individual goals conflict with team goals. In the ABA, individual goals and team goals were mutually-supporting: If an individual player wanted to make it to the NBA, as a team we had to win.

A team-first attitude actually supported each individual player's goals.

We win—they win. We all win: As individuals and as a team.

So let's talk about goals. Rule number one where goals are concerned: *Never* hide your goals. Goals are meant to be shared. Everyone on the team must know everyone else's goals.

Keep in mind I don't feel personal goals must be shared. But team goals—or individual goals that contribute or impact team goals—must be shared. For example, if I ask a player to state his primary goal, there is really only one right answer: "To make my teammates better."

Why is that the right answer? If I make the people around me better as a team we will be more successful. If I focus only on making myself a better player, as a team we will fail.

Rule number two: There is nothing wrong with failure. "Failure" is based on an initial definition of success. The key is to determine your personal definition of success.

Say you evaluate two baseball players. Both reach base 100 times. One attempts three steals and is successful each time. His success rate is 100%.

The other attempts to steal 50 times and is successful 40 times. His success rate is 80%.

Evaluating success based on a metric like "success rate" indicates the first player was more successful. But which player would you prefer on your team: The player who advanced to the next base 40 times or the player who was statistically perfect but in practice much less useful to the team?

In business, I'll take the employee who tries 50 new things and succeeds 40 times over the employee who never tries anything new. Failure is a by-product of trying to do a better job. Failure is a by-product of pushing the envelope. Failure is part and parcel of making improvements. I love employees who try and fail. (Make all the mistakes you want—just never make the same mistake twice.) Employees who take calculated, reasonable, informed risks actively seek to improve the company and improve themselves.

If you stand still you may not fail, but you will eventually be left behind.

Rule number three: Individual goals must be team-supporting goals. Sure, one of your personal goals may be to get promoted. That's fine. Moving up in the organization is an admirable goal. But getting promoted is not a team goal. A team goal is completing a project, winning a new customer, re-designing an existing process, or developing cost savings. You may accomplish any one of those tasks as an individual but the result improves the team and the company as a whole.

Individual goals must be team goals.

Personal goals are also fine, but they should not be shared, at least not in a group setting.

Think about it in basketball terms. Say I'm a high school player and my goal is to improve my free-throw average to 90%. Doing a better job at the free-throw line is an individual goal, since when I stand at the line I'm by myself. I either succeed or fail on my own. Shooting free-throws is an individual task. But the goal of becoming a better free-throw shooter is also a team goal, because when I score I help the team win games. If I am a better free-throw shooter I improve the team—and that improvement does not come at the expense of the team or at the expense of any other individual player. In this case my individual improvement also benefits the team.

Now say I'm a high school player and my goal is to someday reach the NBA. That's an individual goal and in large part a personal goal; everything depends on how I choose to pursue that goal.

If I focus on padding my statistics in hopes college coaches will be more likely to notice me—but I do so to the detriment of the team—then my individual goal will negatively impact the team's goal of winning.

If, on the other hand, I realize the best way to move to the next level is to make my teammates better, then my individual goal supports the team's goal. It's a subtle distinction but an important one. In that case, saying, "I want to be the best basketball player I can be, and I want to do that by helping my teammates become better players," is a great way to share an individual goal. Saying, "I want to make it to the NBA and I'll do whatever it takes to get there," automatically sounds selfish.

If one of your goals is to someday become CEO by whatever means necessary, keep that particular goal to yourself (and take a long look in the mirror.) If your goal is to someday become CEO and you plan to get there by working hard, learning as much as you can, and leading teams to achieve company goals, great: Talk about your goals in terms of specific individual or team achievements. Those achievements will eventually build the foundation for your career success. Achieving individual goals that support company goals will not only gain you the respect of your peers and get you noticed by people at higher levels, but will, over time, earn the promotions you seek.

So let's put goal-setting and goal-sharing into practice. Here's what we do at Dynamic Drinkware.

First, we write down our goals. I write down my goals for the day, for the week, and for the month. (I write a lot of stuff down—I have a good memory, but notes beat memory every time.) Everyone else writes down their goals as well.

Then we share our goals. At the end of each week we discuss our goals from two perspectives.

First, every person discusses whether or not he or she met the goals they listed and shared the previous week. If they met their goals, that's great. We move on. If not, we discuss why those goals were not achieved and more importantly what specifically we can do to ensure those goals are achieved.

Then each person shares their goals for the next week.

By sharing individual goals we not only have a better understanding of team and company activities but more importantly we find ways to help each other reach our goals.

If I don't know what you are working on, how can I help you?

Years ago I worked for Purolator's delivery division. We were a ground carrier and an air carrier (in fact, we were the first integrated carrier to provide services similar to what companies like FedEx now provide.) The company decided to expand service capabilities by offering what we called an extended ground service. The idea was to pick up and deliver larger items a trucking company would typically handle and deliver those items around the country within days rather than weeks.

The basic premise was to leverage our existing freight carrier capabilities to capture a larger slice of the package and delivery market. We already had the tractor-trailers and basic infrastructure in place...so why not use our existing capabilities in a different way? We called the new project Operation Bootstrap.

My job was to find an enabling customer to kick-start the initiative. I looked for a customer with needs matching the service we hoped to offer. After some digging I found a company that supplied equipment to fast food restaurants: They manufactured tables, desktops, laminates, counter-tops, and large cabinets—they manufactured a variety of capital items used to outfit new restaurant locations. Since their production facilities were local, we could easily modify our ground-hub system to sort and stage items for distribution to locations around the country.

I worked out the details and our first shipment was from Columbus, Ohio to Denver, Colorado. I determined it would take us five to seven days to deliver the shipment, a time frame the customer was more than happy with. Great!

Well, maybe not so great. We were off and running... but disaster was already bubbling below the surface. Different teams within Operation Bootstrap had not communicated with each other. As a result, instead of picking up items, staging them, and placing them on tractor-trailers for delivery to Denver in five to seven days, the company brought in four jumbo-jets to pick up and deliver everything overnight.

We simply didn't communicate. Other teams within Operation Bootstrap assumed we were doing business as usual... and "business as usual" meant overnight service where our freight delivery folks were concerned. We lost thousands and thousands of dollars on the program due to a basic mistake and misunderstanding. Sure, the delivery time greatly exceeded customer expectations... but we took a financial beating.

My team knew what it was doing... and the air freight team knew what it was doing... but *they* didn't know what *we* were doing. We did not function as a team—we functioned as separate entities with separate goals. Our goal was to deliver the shipment in five to seven days. Their goal was to deliver the shipment overnight. All we had to do was share our respective goals.

But we didn't.

That's why I'm such a stickler for communication in general and for sharing goals in particular. I was part of a team that learned a $250,000 lesson—you can guarantee I'll never forget it. (In fact, the word "overnight" sometimes still makes me cringe.)

Communication is why coaches call time-outs. Time-outs aren't used to assert control or to yell at players (although sometimes yelling does occur.) Time-outs are simply the best way to communicate with the players as a team. How can you set up a play if you don't call a time-out? How can you put strategies in place if you don't call time-out? How can you put contingency plans in place if you don't call a time-out? How can you slow down your opponent's momentum if you don't call a time-out?

Time-outs in basketball are like meetings in a corporate setting. Meetings are used to communicate, to share details, to share goals, and to make sure everyone is on the same page. So are time-outs.

I've played on a lot of teams. My coaches went over goals on every team I ever played on, all the way back to 7th grade basketball and even to youth league. Most of the time our team goals were simple: Come to practice, work hard, support your teammates, and maintain a good attitude. Individual goals were often simple, too: Make better decisions, share the ball, involve teammates more, and take smarter shots. My coaches shared goals because they wanted us to buy into those goals. As a result every player knew the team's goals.

That's why I ask each person on our team to share their goals for the next week and to share what they achieved that week. I want us all to know where we're going...and how we, as a team, will get there.

In our meetings, I don't care to hear about itineraries. I'm interested but ultimately don't care about your travel plans or your daily schedule. Your itinerary is "how" you will achieve your goals. I want to know your goals. I want to know "what" you plan to accomplish. As a team we all need to know what you will accomplish, just like you need to know what the rest of us will accomplish.

If our goals mesh, we can work on achieving them together. If I can help you achieve your goals, I will. I work for you. But I can't help you, and you can't help me, unless we know each other's goals.

When an employee does not reach his or her goals, I don't ask a lot of questions about what happened. I want to know how I can help. Everyone in the room should want to help. That is the true definition of a team: People committed to helping each other—and the team—reach its goals.

But to know how we can help, we need to know your goals.

Share your goals. And then do everything you can to reach them—even during times of change.

Eight

Change

Have you ever painted the wrong house?

No?

I have.

When I was young I looked up to a lot of people. I especially looked up to the older basketball players in the area. I wanted to play like them. I wanted to *be* like them.

I still look up to people. I try to model my behavior after successful people. The best way to learn is to see what successful people do—and do what they do.

The second best way to learn is to see what unsuccessful people do—and avoid doing what they do.

In the 8th grade I looked up to a few of the boys in the neighborhood who were seniors in high school. They were great basketball players, and I wanted to be able to play like them. They also painted houses in the summertime to make money, and a friend and I naturally decided we would paint houses, too. We planned to paint houses during the day and play basketball in the evening. Of course I was also working at our family's ice cream store. I was more than willing to be a very busy guy.

We started by looking for customers, which turned out to be fairly easy. We lined up four or five customers within the first couple of days. My friend found an older lady who wanted her house painted right away, and she said she would give us a bonus to paint her house first. We thought that was awesome—our first days in business and customers were already paying us bonuses!

So, on that fateful day, we got started bright and early. I was due at the ice cream store at 9 a.m., so we needed to get started as soon as we could. The sun was barely up, the birds were starting to chirp, and there we were, on our ladders, painting the second story. (Like all good painters, we started at the top of the house and planned to work our way down.)

Then we heard the front door open. We glanced down and instead of seeing the nice older lady who hired us, an older gentleman stepped out, looked up, and said loudly, "Boys, what the heck are you doing up there?"

Turns out we were painting the wrong house. We were supposed to paint the house across the street.

So I got out of the house painting business.

Don't get me wrong: We finished painting his house. That was the right thing to do. Whether he had asked us to or not, we started the job and we needed to finish it. That was never in question. We also did it for no charge and he didn't furnish the paint, which definitely cut into my ice cream money.

My friend decided to keep painting houses, but I did not. In hindsight I should not have gotten into the house painting business in the first place. I already had my job in the ice cream store and was not able to put in the time to make sure all the little details were taken care of in a new business... little details like making sure we painted the right house.

I know it's a cliché, but the only thing certain in life and in business is change. Customers will change. Technologies will change. Strategies will change. I think change, and adapting to change, is what makes business fun. Making adjustments and changing directions can certainly be challenging and stressful but it can also be a lot of fun.

I have to admit I'm probably less resistant to change because of my years in basketball. As a player and as a coach I went into every game with a plan. Sometimes we were able to win based on following our initial plan, but good teams recognize your strategies and tactics and make adjustments to take you out of your game plan. As a coach my goal was to keep the other team from doing what it liked and wanted to do. If the other team thrived on transition baskets, we focused on getting back quickly. If the other team liked to pound the ball inside, we focused on denying the entry pass and at times double-teaming their big man.

And, of course, at the same time we focused on doing what we do best. And if they made adjustments to our tactics, we adapted. Doing the same thing and expecting different results is crazy. It doesn't work. Doing the same thing and expecting different results is what I call the "hope" plan: "Boy, they're killing us...I sure *hope* it works this time...."

Trust me. If it didn't work last time, it won't work this time either.

In basketball identifying the changes necessary during a game can sometimes be easy. (Next time you watch a game, try to spot changes the coaches and players have made to their original game plan. But don't let the TV commentators lead you astray...some "experts" know what they're talking about, while others speak just to have something to say.)

Pretend you are a coach and the other team runs the pick and roll. If they are killing you with jump shots, your players will have to go over the screens to defend the jump shot. (Of course, that also means the player has an easier lane to the basket.) If you're giving up lay-ups, your defenders need to go under the screens. If the other team has a great shooter, you may go over the screens so you can stay on the shooter; if he gets substituted, you may decide to stay under the screens to deny drives to the basket. A good pick and roll team forces you to give up something: You can defend the outside shot or defend layups, but you can't deny both. Something has to give—what "gives" depends on what is working for the other team and what adjustments you must make as a result.

Or say the other team tries to create mismatches by going to a bigger lineup. If your guards are small, you can't sit in a zone. You have to adapt. You may go to a man-to-man defense, use your quickness, defend hard, rotate well, and maintain constant ball pressure. If those adjustments work, the other team will adapt. Maybe they will go small and you'll have to go back to a zone to defend the perimeter. The only guarantee is that you will constantly make adjustments throughout the game based on changes in game situations and player substitutions.

Oh—and don't forget making changes due to fouls, injuries, player fatigue....

As a coach you can't control the game. You can't *control* what the other team does but you can certainly *adapt* to what the other team does.

As a coach, your job is to adapt to change and make the right changes.

As a leader, your job is to adapt to change and make the right changes.

Earlier we looked at the value of video study where sports are concerned. In business, when you lose a deal you can't go back and look at the video, but you can ask the customer what you could have done differently. You can ask your team what they felt went wrong. You can create your own "video" by asking questions and looking for answers. Then, the next time you get the chance, go in with a new plan based on what you learned. Make adjustments based on what *didn't* work last time.

Understand I fully realize a lot of times winning business comes down to price. Whether you win a contract is often based in large part on price considerations. Salespersons deal with price negotiations all the time. Customers love to say something to the effect of, "We pay .25 per unit with our current supplier. Your price is .26. I can't give you the business until you come down to at least .25 per unit."

What do you say in response? Sometimes the answer is yes, sometimes the answer is no. First you must think about what may happen the next time; if today you go to .25, next time .24 will be the customer's top price.

Our salespeople try to apply creative solutions to price negotiations. If we decide to lower a price, we look for compromises. Possibly the customer will agree to pay outstanding invoices more quickly. Or possibly we will agree to deliver product at a later date. If we—or you—simply reduce price, the buyer will assume:

◀ The price was too high to begin with, and you hoped to take advantage, and

◀ There is probably even more room left to negotiate

Where price considerations are concerned, making changes may be necessary—but only if you make smart changes.

I learned that lesson the hard way. Years ago I met with a buyer at for Wal-Mart, the world's biggest retailer. We developed what we felt was a beautiful product, and the buyer agreed. In fact, he wanted to order 1.5 million units, but with a catch: He asked me to reduce our price from

38.5 cents to 38 cents per unit. I was young and inexperienced, and the size of the order was incredibly exciting (and I already was picturing how fun it was going to be to call the order in to the office), so I immediately said, "Yes, we can do that!"

The buyer wasn't so quick to make a deal. He said, "Our philosophy is to get the very price for the products we purchase. You immediately went down .05 cents without hesitation or discussion. How do I know that's your best price?"

It turns out I couldn't win the deal because I was not able to convince the buyer that .38 was in fact our best price. It was our best price, but I could not convince him. I was too quick to say, "Yes, I can go down in price," before I thought about the repercussions.

I walked away with my tail between my legs…and having learned a lesson I have never forgotten.

By the way: Contrary to popular belief, Wal-Mart is one of the easiest customers in the world to work with. As long as you say what you will do and then do what you say, everyone at Wal-Mart is easy to work with. If you don't do what you say…Wal-Mart is really tough to work with. And justifiably so: The most expensive real estate in the world is Wal-Mart shelf space. On a dollar per square inch basis, Wal-Mart shelf space is the most expensive real estate in the world. Manufacturers will kill to display their products on Wal-Mart shelves because they know their products will *move*.

Say you claim you will deliver product on Wednesday. If you then don't deliver on time, Wal-Mart is left with empty shelf space. Wal-Mart _hates_ empty shelf space. All retailers hate empty shelf space. Retailers can't sell what they don't stock. In return for your missed delivery, Wal-Mart (or other retailers) may return your merchandise when it does arrive and charge any penalties specified in the contract.

Say what you will do, and do what you will say. Then you'll be okay.

In 1998 our company was selected as one of the vendors of the year by Wal-Mart. I was the Director of Worldwide Sales, but ultimately I had only a small slice of responsibility for our success. Quentin Schonewise was our national sales manager for housewares. I visited the customer occasionally, but Wal-Mart was Quentin's world. He worked the account—_hard_. He met their every need. He made sure product was always on the shelves, helped pick colors, helped Wal-Mart coordinate marketing programs...while our success was based on a total team effort, Quentin led the charge. He wasn't the boss, but he was _the man_. He told Wal-Mart what we would do and we did it.

And Wal-Mart loved us.

Here's the thing about Wal-Mart. Wal-Mart lets their customers be their final judge. The consumer makes the ultimate decision because the consumer buys products they feel have value. Wal-Mart follows an unstated but nevertheless real business premise: Just because an item is inexpensive doesn't mean it can't function well and look good, too. Wal-Mart looks for products they can sell at a low price, in tasteful colors, with a little style...that ultimately provide a lot of value for the money.

Value is the key to every successful product. People will pay for value. People want value. People demand value. Wal-Mart customers are tough customers, so Wal-Mart is a tough customer as well. But in the end all Wal-Mart asks of its suppliers is that they deliver on their promises. Working with Wal-Mart can actually make almost any company perform even better, because meeting Wal-Mart expectations means manufacturing a quality product, meeting delivery schedules, communicating effectively, and providing great customer service. Working with a customer like Wal-Mart is a challenge, sure, but it's a challenge that can make your company better.

One other note about Wal-Mart: Wal-Mart does not want to be its suppliers' largest customer. Wal-Mart often makes deals with large companies specifically because they will not be that company's largest customer. The last thing Wal-Mart wants a company to say is, "Wal-Mart put us out of business." Wal-Mart does not look for companies that will work with Wal-Mart exclusively; Wal-Mart only looks for companies that will do what they say they will do.

If you do what you say you will do, you can meet the needs of almost every customer. If you know you cannot meet a customer's needs, don't say you can. Say what you *can* do, and if what you can do is not good enough, move on. Sometimes the best deal is no deal at all.

Let's go back to dealing with change and making adjustments. If you watch a sporting event on TV you will often hear commentators say, "Hey, you have to dance with the one who brought you." I agree; if it's what has made you successful, by all means dance the same dance with the same partner.

The problem is that whenever you get ready to compete you have already been scouted. Your competition knows a lot about you. I try to know more about our competitors (such as they are) than I know about my own company. I know things their employees do that their managers don't know about. I often know more about their sales strategies because I try to determine the underling themes and tactics; most of their salespeople are at this point functioning on auto-pilot. When you scout another team or another business, it's fun to compete with them because you know what you're up against and can adapt accordingly.

That's why we keep our business quiet. We are often asked by trade magazines to show pictures of our processes, to discuss our manufacturing techniques, and to share how work flows through our plant. We continue to develop exciting, innovative technology, and people are naturally interested. We are flattered by their interest, but we have no reason to advertise our success. Our customers know us— that's all that matters. Many companies want other people to know how successful they are; to me, those companies are the best lead in the world. The more they advertise the more we know. The more they trumpet their successes, the more we learn about how they do business.

So go ahead, if you must, and celebrate in public. Just know your competitors are watching—and they're taking notes. What you say can and will be used against you... in the court of business.

We also typically don't patent products or processes. Quite frankly, in most cases I don't think it's worth the time. If you get to an idea first, and you patent it, in effect your patent tells everyone what you did and how you did it. All they have to do is make a few changes and they're off and running—and competing with you. Sure, you can fight them, but I would much rather fight in the business arena than in the courtroom. I'm not worried about facing competition in the field. We will outwork, out-think, and outhustle our competition in the field.

When you take that approach, patents are irrelevant. (But we do own a few patents. For example, Dynamic Drinkware owns the patent to producing lenticular cups, a patent obtained when we purchased in federal bankruptcy court the assets of Digital Replay, Inc. Today Dynamic Drinkware is the world leader in lenticular cup production.)

In short: Always listen. Never talk. That's how you learn. Don't focus on letting others hear about how wonderful you are—before you know it, you won't be so wonderful anymore. Focus on making changes and adapting to new business environments. Focus on what you can do to make things better.

The speed of light is faster than the speed of sound. At times you can look bright... at least until you are heard.

And don't forget to plan for contingencies. When I was a young coach I called a time-out during a close game to set up our final play. We had the ball and were down a point so I set up an inbounds play for a pick and roll that would lead to a layup or a foul. It seemed like a good plan, since my players were all good free-throw shooters (at least the players I had on the floor were all good free-throw shooters; players who aren't good free-throw shooters don't play at the end of close games.) I felt sure we'd either make a layup or draw a foul—either way we would win.

We passed the ball inbounds and the plan fell apart: The other team had come out in a zone trap defense. I hadn't given my team options or contingencies; I simply assumed my play would work. It didn't.

I was outcoached.

But I also learned from my mistake. I realized I should always consider my options. I should have set up different plays depending on the defense: A play against a trap, a play against a man to man defense, a play against a zone defense...I should have prepared my players for a variety of possibilities so they could adapt to the actual conditions they faced.

The same thing happens in business. Situations change. Situations change you can't control, no matter how hard you try. Instead of trying to re-assert control, a better goal is to develop options ahead of time. What will you do if a delivery is late? What will you do if you fall behind in manufacturing? What will you do if a new competitor enters your market? The key is to not only understand what you want to do; the key is to understand what your opponent or competitor may want to do and have a plan in place to overcome it.

Basketball example: I once coached a very good player. He was big, athletic, and agile. We often worked the ball inside to take advantage of his strengths. One team decided to stop him by, basically, beating on him physically. Every time he caught the ball in the paint the other team hammered him. They had scouted us well, knew what he could do, and decided their only option was to play him extremely physically. He typically scored 24 points a game; at halftime he only had 2 points. He could not get off a shot, much less make one.

At halftime we made adjustments. One was to have him—our big man—bring the ball up the floor. After all, he was a good ball-handler, could shoot mid-range jumpers, and could take people off the dribble. The other team had no idea what to do. Their center could not guard him; he wasn't quick enough. Their point guard couldn't guard him; he was too small. We forced the other team to try to adapt to the adjustments we made, but they weren't able. Sometimes you need to make radical changes in response to changing environments or adjustments your competitors make.

But sometimes the changes required are not so dramatic. When I was the Director of National Sales for a Fortune 500 company I called on a buyer in Chicago. I arrived early for my 3:30 appointment. This buyer had a reputation as a difficult person to deal with and an extremely tough sale. I sat down in his cubicle right at 3:30 and started making my pitch. After a couple of minutes he interrupted, saying, "I need to go to the bathroom."

I waited.

And waited.

And waited.

Thirty minutes went by before another employee walked by and said, "Can I help you?" I explained I was waiting for the buyer to return to his cubicle. The employee said, "Well, you're in for a long wait. He's gone home for the day."

That's right. He bailed on me, without a word.

I was upset but I tried not to let it show. I called him back and left a message. I called again. I kept trying to set up a time to meet with him in his office, but every time I tried he brushed me off.

I finally realized I was doing the same thing, time after time, and expecting different results. What I was doing wasn't working, so the next time I invited him to lunch. He agreed. At lunch he was suddenly calling me "buddy" and "tiger"...he could not have been nicer and friendlier. It turns out he had no interest in seeing me at his office. Lunch? No problem. Making such a small adjustment almost sounds too simple...but that's all it took.

The only terms that matter is customer's terms; you just need to identify those terms so you can make the right adjustments. Think about it. People don't buy from companies. People buy from people. I sat down at my first meeting and jumped right into a business discussion. I tried to steer a ship in water I knew nothing about. I didn't know if the water was cold, hot, deep or shallow. I didn't know if the water was choppy or smooth.

I didn't try to establish a relationship.

People like to help people. People feel good when they can help you. But you have to give them that chance.

Basketball coaches have the chance to make a lot of adjustments during games, but halftime is when the biggest adjustments tend to be made. Why? Because at halftime, coaches have plenty of time to communicate with assistant coaches and players. Most coaches make a lot of halftime adjustments even if their team is winning by a wide margin. Coaches check the stats, especially the other team's stats: Which player is getting a lot of rebounds, which player is getting offensive rebounds, which players are scoring…adjustments start with numbers. If the other team is much bigger and we're getting out-rebounded, our only option may be to run our offense closer to the basket so we can more easily block out. We look for options.

You may not always have great options, but you do always have options.

During a game a close game, if I had time-outs left I always called them. Some coaches hesitate to call time-out at the end of close games, especially if they feel the opponent's defense is so good that they may struggle to inbound the ball after the time-out. I never worried about that. I had confidence we could get the ball inbounds, and I felt taking a time-out helped put our team in a better position.

After all, a coach is paid to coach—so coach. Set something up. Communicate. Put your team in the best position to win.

But I didn't call time-out simply to "freeze" an opposing player getting ready to shoot free-throws. Lots of coaches do, but I didn't. The shooter is expecting you to freeze him. Why meet his expectations? If the player isn't a particularly good shooter, there is no reason to call time-out. Let him wonder why you don't.

Time-outs may look chaotic, but in reality there is an efficient process at work. Often you'll see the head coach and his assistants huddle for a few moments. In effect it's like a quick meeting: One assistant may suggest going to a zone, another assistant may suggest a certain substitution, and another may remind everyone how many time-outs are left.

Since the head coach is responsible for all aspects of the game, often the assistants see things the head coach is not able to see. The head coach has a lot to manage: Players, substitutions, game situations, offense, defense, the officials... the head coach is managing a wide range of game facets. Individual assistants typically have responsibility for tracking specific facets of the game: What plays work, what plays don't work, stats, etc. So the assistants provide input and make brief, to-the-point recommendations.

The head coach quickly sifts through those recommendations and decides what to do. Then he huddles with the players to communicate with the team as a group.

At the end of the time-out you will often see an assistant coach speak briefly with one of the players. That coach may be offering a little personal inspiration or encouragement, but more like he is simply providing individual advice that is not of interest to the entire team.

Every coach's goal: To communicate, to deal with change, and to make adjustments.

That is why a time-out is just like a business meeting.

Time-outs help you win. Time-outs are great opportunities for coaches to coach. Meetings are great opportunities for leaders to lead. Time-outs and meetings are opportunities for winners to adapt and make changes.

Change is good. Change is *great*. Don't wait for change. *Be* the change. As we'll discuss later, there is nothing wrong with change as long as you know what you are changing from, what you are changing to...and what the effect of your changes will be.

Nine

You Thought
Quitting Was Easy

I raced in the finals against an outstanding runner. He was older than me—I was a high school sophomore and he was a senior—and he was definitely more accomplished. Still, in a two-mile race anything can happen, right?

Okay, I'll be honest. Going into the race I felt I had no chance to win. But I love being the underdog, and it was fun to imagine winning just might be possible, so I still went into the race eager to do my best.

I ran just off his right shoulder for seven laps. I pulled up beside him on the final lap, hung tough when he started his kick down the backstretch, and in the final straight was still with him. To his surprise and mine—and to the surprise of everyone else watching—with fifty yards to go I still had a chance!

But I let up.

And I lost.

Immediately after the race a number of people congratulated me on my effort. Everyone was surprised I had come so close to beating him.

One person didn't congratulate me, though. The next day at school one of my teachers, Ms. Nancy Quick, said, "Bob, I don't mind if you lose as long as you have done your best, but yesterday I saw you let up. You quit on us." (As you can tell, I went to high school during a time when teachers could be more honest and less politically correct when talking to their students.)

Her words bothered me—a lot. I was embarrassed.

I was ashamed.

I was hurt.

So I promised myself I would never quit again.

I only lost one other race in high school. In that race I did my best; I simply lost to a better runner. But I never quit. I never gave up. I gave it everything I had, all the way to the line, each and every time.

I am not ashamed to admit Ms. Quick's words hurt me. At the time I felt she kicked me when I was down. Later I realized her willingness to be honest did me a tremendous favor. Today I respect and appreciate her words because they made a tremendous impact on my life. The lesson she taught me has helped me in sports, in business…in all aspects of my life.

She helped teach me to never quit.

I also realized something else just as important. Ms. Quick said I had quit on my teammates, and she was right. I did let the team down. But to make matters worse, I quit on myself. I didn't give 100%, all the way to the end of the race, and I let myself down.

I'd love to race that guy again. I think about it all the time. I know I can't, and there's nothing I can do. But what I can do is give 100% in every other "race" I run, whether at home, in business, or in my community.

Quitting isn't easy. *Trying* is easy. Working hard and giving something your all is easy. When you do your best you have no regrets. A life without regrets is an easy life to live. Quitting is *hard*—because the effects of quitting last a lifetime. Regrets last a lifetime.

I've tried to pass that lesson to our children. Take my son Ryan. (You've already met Brendan.)

Brendan was very interested in athletics. Ryan was more interested in other activities. For example, in 8th grade he earned the lead role in the school play. I played basketball in front of thousands of people, but I would never have dreamed of performing onstage. I was blown away by how he handled the part and by how he handled himself; he was, in a word, spectacular. He is extremely talented; he just wasn't particularly interested in sports. He didn't enjoy baseball, didn't enjoy soccer . . . and of course we didn't make him play any sport he did not want to play.

Then one day he told us he wanted to play football. I was surprised and of course was supportive. But I also explained how joining the football team involved making a commitment to the coaches, to the team, and to himself. He understood, and for a short time really got into it.

A couple weeks later we sat at the dinner table and he was very quiet. Ryan was normally very talkative and animated. He was almost always a fun kid, but not that night.

"What's going on, Ryan?" I asked.

He was silent for a few moments. "It's football," he finally said. "I'm not having much fun."

"Did you get hurt?" I asked.

"No," he replied. "It's not that. It's just not fun. I want to quit."

I told him he couldn't quit. He had joined the team and made a commitment. He explained he was miserable and didn't want to play anymore. We talked for awhile, and finally I said, "Ryan, I won't make you play if you don't want to play. Sports should be fun. I won't make you play."

He was thrilled.

The next day I came home early from work. "It's time to go to practice," I said.

"Wait, Dad. You told me I could quit," he said.

"No. I did not say you could *quit*. I said you did not have to *play*. You joined the team and are still a member of the team. You need to see it through. You don't have to play, but you can't quit. You will go to every practice and game and stand and support your teammates. You made a commitment. You are a part of the team. Now let's go tell the coach what you have decided to do."

So he did. He faced the coach, told him he didn't want to play anymore, and that he would still be a part of the team. He explained that he would go to every meeting, go to every practice, and go to every game. It took a lot of courage for him to face the coach, but he did it.

After the meeting with his coach Ryan went to practices for four or five days, and then decided he wanted to play. He played the rest of the season. He didn't play the next season, but he saw that season through. He didn't quit. He had experienced and learned a life lesson, and I had never been so proud of him.

That's why it's not easy to quit. When you get involved in something you should always see it through. Once you make a commitment, stick with it. Be committed to your teammates and to yourself.

Later, when Ryan was a junior in high school, he decided he wanted to play again. (Keep in mind he hadn't played any other sports since junior high.) We talked and he said he was interested in football because he wanted to be around his friends, the leaders on the football team, and also so he could be involved in another school activity. After a little thought he decided to be the mascot instead, putting his theatrical and performing abilities to good use. As he told me later, "You don't have to be one of the players to be involved with the team."

Later, when he graduated high school, he was accepted at the University of Kansas. After his second semester he wanted to transfer; Kansas is a great school but it had not turned out to be the experience he hoped for. He wanted to transfer to a good business school and narrowed his choices to Texas Christian University (TCU) and Tulane.

He made a few calls.

The folks at Tulane never called back. The wife of the TCU Chancellor called me, his dad, to let me know how much TCU would love to have Ryan as a student and campus leader. (Yes, I was impressed.)

Even so, he was still interested in Tulane, so we went for a visit. We checked out the campus, then went into New Orleans, walked down Bourbon Street, got a drink, and soaked in the atmosphere. I could tell he loved the scene.

"Ryan," I said. "Take a second and look up and down the street. What do you see? Do you see anyone wearing a Green Wave shirt? I don't. Bourbon Street is fun. New Orleans is fun. But Bourbon Street is not college."

He decided to enroll at TCU, and once there joined the Phi Kappa Phi fraternity. As a community service effort Phi Kappa Phi worked with kids with disabilities. One of their major activities was the Journey of Hope, a cross-country bicycle trip designed to raise money and awareness for the cause. He wanted to participate in the Journey of Hope.

The problem was he had not ridden a bicycle in about fifteen years. He didn't even own a bike. Plus he needed to line up sponsors.

I wasn't worried about whether he would find sponsors. I did worry about whether he could cycle across the country, though.

We went to a sporting goods store and I helped him choose a bike. The day we brought the bike home, Ryan fell off the bike in the driveway; when he stopped he forgot his feet were still clipped into the pedals. But God bless him. He worked hard and trained every day to get ready for the trip.

In June Susan and I flew to San Francisco for the Journey of Hope kickoff banquet. A number of people spoke to the crowd, but I only remember one thing.

"If you think you know your sons now," one speaker said, "Trust me. You won't know them when they finish the Journey of Hope."

I watched as he rode over the Golden Gate Bridge to start the trip. For the next few months his group rode between 35 and 120 miles a day. They set out early in the morning, rode to a new city, and worked with kids with disabilities in that city before heading out the next day to do it all over again. The group was followed by a van carrying supplies, but the van also served as a "broom wagon." If a rider got too tired, the van would sweep him up, rack his bike, and drive him to the next stop.

Ryan didn't want to be "racked," so he rode: Over mountain ranges, across plains, for hundreds and hundreds of miles, completing the entire length of the trip.

The Journey of Hope ended in Washington, D.C. on the steps of the Capitol. My wife, my mother and I met him there, proud of his physical accomplishment but more proud of his service. His group of seventy riders raised over $335,000 and spent time with thousands of children with disabilities. He didn't quit—and he gave back to people less fortunate.

I could not have been more proud. The speaker at the event kickoff in San Francisco was right. The trip had a profound experience on Ryan and on all of his teammates. He was not the same boy we watched depart from San Francisco; he came back a man.

Later, at TCU Ryan started an organization called Rise School for college kids to spend time with disabled children in the area.

Looking back, I know Ryan received more from taking part in the Journey of Hope than the charity received from his efforts. He made a public and a personal commitment, didn't quit, and made a real difference. Quitting might have seemed easy...but think about what he would have lost if he had taken the "easy" way out.

It's also "easy" to quit in the business world.

Take sales. Lots of salespeople call on a customer and don't get the order. Hearing the word "no" is an everyday occurrence for most salespeople. "No" is a fact of life in the sales profession. (If you never hear the word "no," you are taking orders, not selling.)

Quitting, however, does not have to be a fact of life.

When I joined Purolator Courier I went through a fairly extensive sales training program. Near the end of the process I was assigned to one of the top salesmen. I was told he was the best in the business and I could learn a lot from him.

Sounded good to me!

So I rode with him for four days, making sales calls. Early on he gave me fairly direct advice. My job in sales meetings was to be quiet. I wasn't to open my mouth unless he specifically called on me. I was the trainee so I followed instructions. After each customer visit he conducted a debriefing of sorts, talking about what happened in the meeting and giving me pointers on how to handle different situations.

I saw right away he had a very direct sales style. He was brash, to the point, and aggressive. He took charge and commanded meetings. His personality was different from mine, and I wasn't sure I could completely model myself after him (or that I even wanted to model myself after him), but I did know I could learn from him. He was one of the company's best salespeople. Learning what to do from the best in the business is always a smart move.

One day we called on a buyer and the meeting quickly went downhill. My mentor was confrontational, questioned everything the buyer said, pushed for information and agreement... and the buyer grew more and more frustrated and agitated. Finally the buyer exploded.

"Get out," he said, "And stay out!"

My mentor said, "That's fine. We'll go. Oh—and thanks for your hospitality," he added with more than a touch of sarcasm.

We got in the car and started to drive away. My mentor was quiet for a few moments, then turned to me and said, "You know, I think that call went pretty well."

"What?" I replied. "He threw us out!"

"Yes, he did throw us out," he said, "but he also listened. He may not have liked everything I said, but he did hear what I said. Plus, always remember this: "'No'" means 'maybe.' 'Maybe' means 'yes.'"

I thought he was crazy, but I didn't say so.

That Friday we had our scheduled sales call. All salespersons participated in a weekly conference call. Each sales rep shared their results for the week with each other and with the Vice President of Sales. My mentor was the last to speak.

"We had a great week," he said. "We found a new customer that will give us a big chunk of business."

I couldn't believe it. We hadn't made any sales—much less to the buyer he was referring to.

"Tell us about the customer," our VP said.

"Well, I don't have all the details yet, but I did get two orders: Get out and stay out."

The VP didn't think it was funny.

After the call I asked my mentor why he had been so confident about winning business from a customer who threw us out.

"It's a great opportunity," he said. "Sure, he threw us out, but he remembers me. He knows who I am. I guarantee he's thought about our meeting. When I call him back, at least he will know who I am."

To my surprise, thirty days later he landed a $1.6 million contract from that buyer.

"Here's the thing," my mentor explained later. "*He* actually returned my call. He knew we could help him, and he asked me to work out the details so the deal made good business sense for his company. He said he called me because most people who get kicked out of a meeting would never have the courage to call back. He may not have liked the way the meeting went, but now he knows I will be there if times get tough. Anybody can walk away and never come back—it takes guts to get thrown out and come back for more."

My mentor also taught me that the sales profession is a lot like baseball. Two strikes is no big deal. "Get out" and "stay out" is only two strikes. You only strike out when "get out" and "stay out" is followed by "and never come back."

Viewed from a different perspective, in effect he used a strategy some basketball coaches use. Occasionally a coach will purposely draw a technical foul in order to change the atmosphere of a game: To get the crowd involved, to get players involved...a confrontation with a referee is rarely helpful in and of itself, but at times there can be other benefits.

I learned from my mentor at Purolator, but I didn't adopt all of his techniques. I also can't say I have never slipped.

Years later I was a Director of National Sales. I called on SuperValu, at the time the largest grocery store chain in the country. The buyer paid almost no attention during my presentation. Our meeting felt like a complete waste of time.

In fact, he seemed so disinterested I didn't even follow up afterwards.

Two weeks later he called. "Hey, Bob," he said, "why haven't I heard from you since our meeting?"

I didn't know what to say—I was surprised he even remembered me. Fortunately he filled the silence, saying, "We've awarded your company the bid. Congratulations!"

I was stunned. I had no idea he would give us his business—I had no idea he even heard a single word I said during the presentation. But he was listening. He had played his cards close to his vest, poker faced, intentionally giving me no indication of his level of interest. I got the business, but not because I did my job well.

In business, "no" means "maybe."

"Maybe" means "yes."

I thought my presentation bombed, so I quit. I took my ball and went home.

What a wake-up call. I thought I knew the answer...but I didn't know the answer.

"No" means "maybe." In a business setting, the word "no" only means "no" if you quit. Quitting isn't easy. Quitting is in fact an incredibly hard thing to do...especially if you consider what will happen when you quit.

When you give up and fail to do the best you can, you give away the opportunity to succeed.

I wish I could race that guy from high school guy again. Sadly, I won't get the chance. (But I have raced him thousands of times in my mind.) If I had given my all I may still have lost...but today I would not give that race a second thought.

Stick with it and see it through.

When you do your best you are left with no regrets.

That is why quitting is *hard*.

Ten

Team Balance
is Everything

As our coach liked to say, they looked like guys who bounce the ball and miss the floor.

(He also liked to say, "Those guys couldn't play dead in a cowboy movie." He did like his sayings.)

In this case, he was right. Our opponents looked horrible while they warmed up. No one on the team looked at all athletic: They had no quickness, no speed, and no real coordination. I have to admit we were laughing—quietly, to ourselves—as we watched them run through pre-game drills.

Everything changed when the game started. Each player may not have been individually talented, but each player played well within their system, knew his role, defended well, communicated well...individually they were mediocre but as a team they were talented. They gave us everything we could handle.

Competing against them taught me two lessons.

One, never underestimate your opponent. Look for advantages, look for weaknesses, but always be cautious, never assume...and always adjust to the reality of the competition you face.

The second lesson I learned? Individual ability is great—but if you want to win, team play and team balance is *everything*.

You can have an outstanding scorer, or a great rebounder, or an amazing point guard on your team...but if you don't have all the ingredients, you won't win.

Think about it this way. The last few years the Kansas City Chiefs have missed the playoffs. In addition to head coach Todd Haley, the Chiefs have brought in superstar coaches like offensive coordinator Charlie Weiss (most recently head coach at Notre Dame) and defensive coordinator Romeo Crennel, former head coach of the Cleveland Browns.

That's a high-powered coaching staff...but without great players, the Chiefs will struggle to win. "There are no winning jockeys on three-legged horses."

Or look at it from a different perspective: Send me off to coach the Lakers and we will win. Send me off to coach the Nets and we'll probably get our butts kicked.

In business, I can take a project to the moon with the right team. But I must have the whole package in place; we won't succeed without all the parts in place.

In basketball terms, all coaches want great shooters on their team. Defense is important and wins championships, but still, if you don't score, you can't win. But, as I mentioned earlier, ask a great coach if he wants five great shooters on his team, and he'll say no. If you have five great shooters you have four problems. Dr. Naismith only gave us one ball. With five shooters, one guy is happy—the rest are not.

The same is true in business. Combine a stellar sales force with inefficient manufacturing and you will generate lots of orders but will ship few products. Combine an efficient manufacturing team with a sub-par distribution group and it doesn't matter how far ahead of schedule manufacturing can get—if you don't deliver on time, to the right destination, as an organization you have failed.

Every role, no matter how low on the organizational chart, is crucial. In fact, I like to evaluate companies by their receptionists. Sound crazy, granted, but it almost always works. One phone call to a receptionist will tell you a lot about a company. If he or she is professional, courteous, friendly, and upbeat, that tells me a lot. A bad receptionist not only creates a terrible first impression, he or she also reveals a lot about the company's leadership. No good manager or leader will put up with a poor receptionist. Good leaders recognize many people perceive the receptionist as the face of the company. Good leaders won't allow an unprofessional, discourteous, or negative person to represent the company or themselves.

If a leader will allow an unprofessional person to represent the company, you can bet that leader is less than professional as well.

I also glance at the cars in the employee parking lot. I do a quick scan of makes, models, and condition—the cars the employees own tell you an awful lot about the success of the company.

Teams play to the personality of their coaches. Business teams "play" to the personality of their leaders. Take basketball teams. A basketball team definitely plays to the personality of its coach. Bob Huggins is intense, driven, and fiercely competitive. He is more than willing to get in a player's face if necessary. His teams play that a way too: They play with fire and intensity and seek to physically dominate their opponents. Mike Krzyzewski is a tough guy; his teams also play tough.

A team like Gonzaga plays a more laid-back game. Their coach, Bob Few, is fiercely competitive but has a calmer, more relaxed approach to managing his players and a game. (His approach works, too: For the last twelve years his teams have won 80% of their games.) Bob's teams are a reflection of his personality.

By the way: Great coaches may use different approaches, but they do share two things in common.

They create team balance.

And they win.

Great companies create team balance too. Pick a successful company: What are its employees like? Southwest Airlines is known for great flight attendants, ground crews, and customer service employees. Leaders set the tone and expect teams to follow that tone. Want to know what a particular leader is like? Check out his or her people. You'll learn everything you need to know. Over time, teams become a reflection of their leaders—for good or for bad.

Over time a leader's personality spreads and becomes pervasive. Say you are a leader. Employees will mimic your actions, but if you share information, share team goals, ensure that everyone in the group understands their roles and their importance to the organization...when someone goes off track, a number of people will say, "Wait a minute—that's not how we do things here." You won't have to. In sports, coaches like to talk about players who are leaders in the locker room. Those leaders act as an extension of the coach.

The same thing can happen in business—if you let it. The key is to create balance.

I often think of things in basketball terms. Just as in an organization, there are a number of important roles that must be filled on a basketball team. The parallels are pretty easy to spot:

Point Guard	Purchasing
Shooter	Production
Rebounder	Accounting
Defender	Engineering
Enforcer	Sales & Marketing

6th Man	Shipping
Free-Throw Shooter	Customer Service
Team Manager	Receptionist
Coach	Owner/Manager

You can switch the roles around if you like, but the overriding analogies should be obvious. Purchasing is like a point guard, distributing the "ball," making sure every department has what it needs, etc. Production "scores" by manufacturing a quality product; to the consumer, the product is the tangible result of the company's efforts, just like making a basket is a tangible result of a basketball team's efforts. Accounting does the dirty work, so to speak, cleaning up the boards, making sure mistakes are corrected, taking care of all the little details, and "boxing out" by meeting all legal and regulatory requirements. The Owner/Manager is listed last. As a leader, your employees don't work for you; you work for your employees. The buck may stop with you, but you should always consider yourself to be at the bottom of the totem pole.

If one function slips or comes up short, the entire team suffers.

Without balance the entire team, over the long run, will fail.

As a leader, your responsibility is to create balance. Your job is to find the right players, put them in the right roles, and turn them loose.

But occasionally you will need to nudge people along. I once hired an employee who was sharp, talented, and clearly a good fit for the position and for our company. But I noticed he was struggling to fit in. He didn't eat with the rest of the team, didn't hang out with others…he was reserved and seemed to stay in a little shell.

I brought him in my office for a casual chat. "How are you doing?" I asked. "I may be wrong, but it doesn't look like you're having a lot of fun."

He said he didn't feel accepted by the team. He didn't feel other people were including him in the normal give-and-take of office conversations and activities.

I said, "We can solve this pretty quickly. I know you are the right guy for the job. You have all the technical skills necessary. But if you want to fit in, you have to put in a little effort. Fitting in with the team is not a one-way street. If you just sit in a corner, don't assume people will seek you out… because they won't. To *have* a friend you first have to *be* a friend. "

So he did. He changed his demeanor almost instantly. The rest of the team loved him, and he had a lot more fun at work. We depended on him not just for his abilities but also for the intangible qualities he brought to the team.

He just needed a little nudge. Little nudges, when you're a leader, are your job.

Balanced teams have room for role players. To play in high school and even in college, you have to do some things pretty well, but not a lot: Dribble, pass, rebound, shoot, and defend. If you can do those things well you will go far—at those levels. If you want to be a pro player, you don't have to do everything well, but you do have to do one thing great.

Dennis Rodman was a great rebounder—there was a place for him on the team. Or take a current player: Ron Artest has a broad range of skills and does a lot of things well, but most importantly he is an outstanding defender. The Lakers have plenty of guys who can score; they don't need another scorer. Artest's defensive abilities add balance to the team. He does one thing uncommonly well—so there's a place for him.

Now let's look at team balance form an employee's point of view, since most of us are both leaders and followers. Everyone has a boss, even if your boss is your customer. We all lead people and are in turn led by others.

Kids will often say to me, "Coach, I know I'm not the most talented player on my team. I probably never will be. What can I do to be more valuable? What can I do to be more important to the team?"

It's a great question, and one people in business should be asking themselves all the time. I often use my son Brendan as an example to answer the question. As you know, Brendan played for Bob Huggins at the University of Cincinnati. While he was not the type of player who would ever win a game (or lose a game) for the team, he could study hard, show up every day with a great attitude, lead by example, and try to out-work everyone else in practice. By doing so, he made his teammates better. That was his role on the team: To do everything he could to make his teammates, and his team, better. He helped make the first-team players better.

Not everyone can be the star, but everyone can be a valuable part of the team.

When I was coaching I was very direct with players and their parents. At the beginning of the season, during our first meeting, I said, "We will never talk about playing time—or, more to the point, your child's lack of playing time. Here's how it works: The five best players may not play. The five players that *play together* the best will play.

"If you want to be a member of this team but you don't think you can handle the fact you might not be one of the five guys who play the most, you probably should leave now. You'll be happier if you find somewhere else to play. I want you to have fun; if you don't have fun you will be miserable and we will be miserable. We are all equal and we are all important. If you are not playing a lot you are in some ways even more important to the team because I can find lots of guys who are willing to play... it's a lot tougher for me to find guys who are willing to work hard in practice and NOT play."

Of course I did everything I could to reward the role players. I got them into games whenever possible. I found times they could play with the starters. Be creative—find ways to recognize your role players. They deserve it.

In business, you may not to be the star. You may not get the glory, the recognition, or the accolades. But without you, the team can't succeed. Every employee contributes. Remember, it's not important to add years to your life but to add life to your years.

Balance is *everything*.

Eleven

Attitude is the Answer

Your attitude determines your altitude.

My younger brother Kevin's attitude certainly determined his altitude.

Kevin was a decent football player, but certainly not a star. He earned a spot on the junior varsity basketball team mainly because he played good defense. Like me he played make-believe baseball games in our backyard, but sometimes it seemed he could toss the ball up in the air ten times and never hit it.

I'm not knocking him—we are all born with different strengths, and athletic ability certainly isn't everything in life. Kevin just wasn't a natural athlete.

But in junior high school he realized he could run well. He went out for track in eighth grade and ran a 2:04 half-mile, a record time at his school. Still, the time he ran in an otherwise forgettable race doesn't really matter. What does matter is that Kevin found his niche. He knew he would not be a star football or basketball player, but he did find out he could run—and run well.

He worked and worked and worked to be the best runner he could possibly be. He lost weight, dropping from 170 to 135 pounds. As a sophomore he finished ninth in the state cross country meet and was named to the all-Ohio team. As a junior he never lost a dual meet race. In fact, all these years later (37, to be precise), he still holds the high school and county two-mile record.

He was poised for an outstanding senior year of high school and had started to think about running in college…and then he contracted mononucleosis. He wasn't able to run his senior year, which meant he disappeared completely from the radar screens of college cross country and track coaches.

But he didn't let a major setback derail him. Through the grapevine, Kevin heard another local runner had received a scholarship offer from Edinboro University in Pennsylvania. He was happy for the other athlete but also frustrated since as a junior he had beaten this individual several times. He called the coach at Edinboro and said, bluntly, "I can run for you. Nothing against Larry (the other runner), but if you think he's a better runner than me, you are wrong."

Edinboro offered Kevin a scholarship. He became a six-time All-American, led Edinboro to national championships in 1975 and 1976, placed second in the cross country national championships and lost by a step to an Olympic runner from Kenya. After college Kevin continued to compete and became one of the top marathoners in the country for Team Nike. He was a finalist in the U.S. Olympic Trials in 1980 and ran a 2:14 marathon.

Kevin is proud of his accomplishments, but I think he is most proud of the fact he did everything he possibly could to reach his dreams. He never quit. He wasn't particularly athletic, but he found a sport he could excel in as long as he was willing to work hard.

After college he became an outstanding teacher and coach. He was inducted into the Teaching Hall of Fame in Dublin, Ohio, the Edinboro University Athletic Hall of Fame, and the Eastlake North High School Athletic Hall of Fame.

Kevin had dreams.

We all have dreams.

Most of us aim high. Whether we reach those heights depends on our attitude. The altitude Kevin reached was based on working, overcoming, persevering, and never quitting. He found a dream his attitude could help him reach. (As you can tell, I'm proud of him for what he has accomplished, both individually and as a teacher and coach.)

When I was young, radio disc jockey Kasey Kasem hosted the weekly radio show *America's Top Forty*. He signed off every broadcast by saying, "Keep your feet on the ground and keep reaching for the stars." All of us reach for the stars, at least in our dreams. Whether you reach the stars depends not on how high you aim but on your attitude. Knowing what you want is important, but determining what you are willing to do is everything.

You can't fly high if you don't aim high. Then, if your attitude is 100%, your altitude will be high. Chase your dreams; whether you reach the sky or not, the work you put in will be worthwhile, in and of itself.

But remember, success is based on the telling the truth: To yourself. When you try to achieve a goal, only you know how hard you worked. Only you know the amount of effort and sacrifice you put in. What other people think doesn't matter—only you know how hard you worked. The worst person to cheat is yourself.

How hard are you willing to work? You get out what you put in; the more you put in, the more you get out. Period. End of story. Pay the premium, reap the benefits.

Keep in mind there is no such thing as instant gratification and there are no shortcuts to real success. Buildings are built one brick at a time. Achieving your dreams is based on assembling a building out of a number of small blocks.

I know people who want to be millionaires. The process of becoming a millionaire starts with earning one dollar, then two, then ten . . . if you get frustrated because you're not a millionaire within the first month or two, you'll never reach your goal. You'll give up.

Any worthwhile endeavor or process takes time. A few of my friends were millionaires, lost everything, and then became millionaires again. They learned the process of making money. What happens along the way from having no money and having millions in the bank is what matters. The journey makes all the difference, and the journey is based on attitude.

Think about lottery winners who end up bankrupt within a few years. It seems impossible to imagine a person could win millions of dollars and wind up drowning in debt, but it happens at an alarming rate. Most did not receive bad advice. Most were not taken advantage of.

In most cases the people who lost it all didn't know how to manage what they had because they had never built a building block by block. They hadn't struggled through the long, hard journey to wealth. People who know how to make money understand what lies between poverty and wealth: They know the steps, they know how to put good people in place, they know how to work together to succeed—they learn, through experience, where each block goes and how to place those blocks securely. A person who becomes rich overnight may be rich...but he or she has never put in the *work*.

You can't always control what happens, but you can control what you do. Your attitude determines what you do—and your attitude determines your altitude.

I'll never forget a basketball game we played in college. We were scheduled to play an away game in an incredibly small gym. Our coach later told a reporter, "Well, the baskets were ten feet high, but it sure was a really small gym...it was so small we had to go outside to change our minds."

As players, we didn't want to play there. In our opinion the gym was too small, too confined, too, well, bush league. We complained to our coach and he said, "Okay. We can always forfeit. But would you rather put a loss on your record or would you rather go to their gym, play your game, and reach high?"

We quickly decided to go into their house and make them wish they had never invited us. We realized we could play the cards we were dealt, or we could fold. We couldn't control the size of the gym, but we could control whether and how we played.

We won because our attitude determined our altitude.

We gave it 100%–and we got 100% in return.

Speaking of 100%; I'm always irritated when I hear people say things like, "I gave 110%."

I'm not a math whiz, but I do know that it is impossible to give more than 100%. If I give it my all, I give 100%. I don't give 110%. What I am really saying, if I *say* I gave 110%, is that normally I give 80 or 90%...but *this time* I gave it my all.

Don't believe me? Here's a little tool I like to use to measure effort. First, each letter represents a number. Think of it as a code:

A	B	C	D	E	F	G	H	I	J	K	L	M	N	O	P	Q	R	S	T	U	V	W	X	Y	Z
1	2	3	4	5	6	7	8	9	10	11	12	13	14	15	16	17	18	19	20	21	22	23	24	25	26

For example, the letter A equals 1, B equals 2, C equals 3, etc.

So let's break a few codes. Here's one; take the words "hard work."

H-A-R-D-W-O-R-K
8+1+18+4+23+15+18+11 = 98%

Hard work is great, but hard work only adds up to 98%. Now another one:

K-N-O-W-L-E-D-G-E
11+14+15+23+12+5+4+7+5 = 96%

Knowledge is important, but knowledge only adds up to 96%.

Let's go in a different direction:

B-U-L-L-S-H-I-T
2+21+12+12+19+8+9+20 = 103%

That's right: Bullshit adds up to 103%...which is impossible. The same is true, to a more extreme degree, with:

A-S-S-K-I-S-S-I-N-G
1+19+19+11+9+19+19+9+14+7 = 118%

What word does add up to 100%? You guessed it:

A-T-T-I-T-U-D-E
1+20+20+9+20+21+4+5 = 100%

Attitude determines altitude. Hard work and knowledge are important. Ass kissing and bullshit are, well, ass kissing and bullshit. Attitude, combined with hard work and knowledge, determines your level of success.

A few years ago I interviewed a very nice young lady for a sales position. She was well-educated, had direct sales experience, demonstrated good interpersonal skills—on paper and in person she appeared to be the total package.

Until she asked about the travel requirements for the job, that is.

I told her I couldn't say for sure how often she would travel. Some weeks she might be on the road for two days, other weeks for five days, and some weeks she wouldn't travel at all. How much she traveled would vary based on customer and company needs.

She said, "Well, that's a problem. In the summer I need to be home every Thursday because of my softball team."

"You manage a softball team?" I asked.

"No, I play rec softball on a co-ed team," she replied.

I said, "So if we need you to be in Los Angeles on Thursday and Friday to meet with an important customer, you wouldn't be able to make the trip?"

"No," she said, "That would interfere with softball. I need to be here on Thursdays."

We didn't hire her. She was a very nice, and I wished her well, but her priorities did not align with ours. We were willing to make a commitment to her; she needed to make a commitment to us in return. As an organization, we were willing to do whatever it took to help her succeed, but she was not willing to do whatever it took to help us succeed.

The key is to make a commitment to yourself that your attitude will determine your altitude. If you have the drive, if you are willing to do whatever it takes, look for a crack in the door and push your way through. At Dynamic Drink-ware, we hire employees who are committed. I don't have to worry about production; our production team is 100% committed to getting the job done. I don't have to worry about engineering; our engineering staff is 100% commit-ted. They don't talk about what they will do—they do it.

Many people want a job but they don't want the responsibility that comes with the job.

Fully committed, "Do whatever it takes" employees are not easy to find—that's why good leaders are always on the lookout for talent. Fortunately, great talent is easy to spot. Simply look at what people have done, where they have been, and why they are leaving their situation. We look for people who have run out of road at their current company; they are looking for more but have reached a dead-end on the road they are traveling. We look for people who want to develop new, fun, exciting products—and want to develop more efficient ways to manufacture those products.

We look for people who want our team to win...and are willing to do whatever it takes to help our team win.

I take the same approach with parents who ask me for advice about how their children can earn college scholar-ships. I tell them success is a lot like getting on an elevator.

When you ride up from the lobby and the doors open, the first floor is filled with "wannabes." It's crowded. Every-one is a wannabe; everyone "wants to be." "wannabe" floor is *huge*.

Let the doors close and ride up to the second floor. The second floor is not as crowded as the first floor, but there are still a lot of people there. The second floor is the "like to be" floor. It's easier to get off the elevator on this floor because there is space available for more people, but there's still not a lot of room.

Stay on the elevator and there is one final floor: The "I need to be" floor. Few people are standing on this floor. There is a ton of room available. Very few people "need to be."

Here's the good news: You get to decide where you get off the elevator. If you want to get off on the "wannabe" floor, you'll join the huge group of other wannabes. The "like to be" floor is also easy to get off on; it's pretty full, but there is definitely room for you. The "need to be" floor is prime real estate: The only people on that floor are the ones who will do whatever it takes.

If you are a wannabe, I can't make you get off on the "need to be" floor. Parents can push their kids off the elevator on the lower floors; only you can decide to get off on the "need to be" floor. In fact, getting off on this floor is not a decision: Getting off is a *need*. If you *want*, you may not do whatever it takes to get the things you want. When you *need*, you will give it your all. You have no choice. You give yourself no choice. You *need* it too badly.

Thinking and doing are two different things. Wanting and needing are two different things.

The same is true if you start or run your own business. You may want to own your own business, but do you *need* to own your own business? Are you driven to run your own business?

Running your own business is almost always very different from being an employee and working for someone else. Let's start with a basic premise and assume there are two basic types of people: Those who work to live, and those who live to work.

Most people work to live. If you start your own business, you may hope to work to live...but to succeed you will almost always need to live to work. (Or else you will probably get frustrated and give up.) Contrary to a lot of popular literature, owning your own business is still almost always a 24–7, nights, weekends, Christmas, Easter, etc. proposition.

Owning your own business is a major commitment—at least if you want to be successful. Along with that commitment must be a willingness to lead people and be surrounded by the right people. If you think you can do everything yourself, you will fail. Every successful business owner relies on experts. Every successful business owner focuses on doing what he or she does best and lets experts do what they do best.

You simply cannot do it all.

And you should not want to do it all. I don't think anyone has lay on their deathbed and said, "You know, I wish I would have worked another hour every day. I really wish I had spent more time at the office."

Instead, most people regret not spending more time with their families, not helping people in the community, not exploring their spirituality...they don't regret not working enough.

Balance is everything.

Attitude determines altitude.

Decide what you want to accomplish—and let nothing stand in your way. Are you a "need to be" person? I hope so!

Twelve

Anyone Can Steer
the Ship When
the Waters are Calm

Picture going home in early November, the holiday season right around the corner...and you just lost your job.

Let's make it worse: You also have a home, kids, responsibilities....

Many people lose their jobs due to poor company results, changes in the economy, a dip in revenue, or simply due to a change in management. Thousands of people around the country are let go every day, through no real fault of their own.

I lost my job that holiday season—but in my case I consider it to have been my fault.

Our company was facing incredibly challenging financial times. Party our struggles were due to increased competition, but we also had decided to change our major focus from ground service to air service. The shift in delivery and business strategy meant the majority of our employees were, unfortunately, no longer needed.

I was young and relatively inexperienced, especially with managing cutbacks and layoffs. As a management team we talked about how to implement the reduction in force. I viewed the situation in fairly simple terms: We had 1,200 employees working in the building. Based on our analysis we would not need more than 250 or 300 of those employees in the near term. I said, "I think the best way to handle this is to identify our best people, and keep them. We should make decisions on who to keep based on the people we think will help us the most as we move forward."

I thought my approach made sense, but the Human Resources team saw things differently. They felt we should base layoffs on seniority, a theoretically more objective but in my mind must less fair and effective approach. Why keep a longer-term mediocre employee when we could keep a shorter-term superstar?

In the end we based our decisions on seniority, and for several days I felt like I was watching managers stand at the door with hatchets, chopping people down. (Layoffs were in fact handled more professionally, but to me that was how the process felt.)

My job was safe, but still I stood off to the side thinking, "Wow—this is hard to watch. The tough times are not likely to be over; eventually it might be me who is forced to walk out that door."

I was golden in my position, I was secure…but I still went ahead and changed jobs just to make a change. I didn't change for more money. I didn't change to advance my career. I just changed to get out of a job I didn't think I liked.

But I didn't do my research and I didn't know enough about my new company.

I knew what I was changing *from* but I didn't know what I was changing *to*.

Always know what you are changing *to*—and why.

Six months later, I realized I had made a huge mistake. At my new company I often disagreed with many of the decisions made. The owners of the business recognized I was not happy and that I was not and would not be able to serve as a committed member of their team. I didn't agree at all with the way the company did business or the way it wished to conduct business in the future. If I had done my homework, I would have realized our philosophies were radically different before I made the change. But I didn't do any homework. I just changed jobs to change jobs.

In the end I didn't leave them—they left me. They cut me loose. My father, when he heard, asked, "Why didn't you do everything you could to bite your tongue and keep your job?"

I could have put the blame on someone else—on *anyone* else—but me, but I didn't. It was my fault: I joined a company I never should have joined.

I replied to my father, "I realize I made a mistake, but I just did not agree with what we were doing. Even if I had kept my mouth shut, I still would have disagreed. I could not in good conscience be part of the team."

The holiday season is a terrible time to find a job, but I have never been one to sit around. I promised my dad, who was justifiably worried about my family, that I would have a job by Thanksgiving. (Reach for the stars, right? Attitude determines altitude.) I combed the classified ads, called friends and colleagues, and came across a listing for a job that sounded interesting.

I submitted my resume, met with the company, liked the industry (even though it was a new industry to me)...and during my interview said, "I'd love to work for you. I am definitely the right guy for the job."

For their part, they respected my work experience, but one interviewer leaned back and said, "Then if you are so good at what you do, why aren't you still doing it?"

His was a fair question. I said, "I researched your industry and your company and I think I can make a real impact. So, I will either work for you or for one of your competitors—who I work for is up to you."

I received an offer two days later and started work the following Monday. I've been in the plastics business ever since.

That time, I knew not only what I was changing from but also what I was changing to. I created pretty choppy professional waters for myself. I had to steer my ship back to calmer waters.

So I know what it feels like to lose my job. Many of us do. I live in an upscale area and I have friends and neighbors who have been "displaced." To a person they are skilled, diligent, great workers with great skill sets...but they have still been out of work.

One person served the same company for almost thirty-five years before he was let go. Another worked in a specific industry and for a time only looked for jobs in that industry. I convinced him to explore other industries, because that's what I had done.

Sure, an interviewer may say (just as one individual said to me), "You don't have industry experience. We're looking for people who have grown up in the business."

Your reply? "I may not have industry experience, but I have lifetime experience. I can bring another vision, another outlook, and another perspective that will work well in your company and your industry. Your team is in the box; I come from outside the box. I'll bring the three Es: Effort, Emotion, and Enthusiasm, and I'll help you make great things happen."

Some of my friends have embraced the opportunity—even though it was forced upon them—to sail into new waters. Others have not embraced that opportunity and unfortunately are still looking for work.

Change can be forced upon you, but sometimes purposely sailing into choppy seas can make you better, too. In fact, people who knowingly steer into choppy seas tend to improve their sailing skills—or find out they shouldn't be sailors at all.

Take the average high school basketball player. Most hope to play basketball in college. Even poor players have hopes and dreams, however unrealistic those dreams may be. I have a soft spot for those kids—while most will stay on the "wannabe" floor, some will ride the elevator to the top, work hard, and through consistent effort and determination make it to the next level. Some will *need* to succeed.

But many kids play what I call "suburban" basketball, and as a result their hopes are unrealistic because they have never truly been tested as players.

If you are a basketball player and you want a realistic evaluation of your skills, go play on the other side of the tracks. Go where the big boys play. Playing against kids your age, with your size, and with your speed tells you little about your actual skill level. Go play with the best in your area. Find the parks where the *real* games are played.

Then you'll see what you're made of.

Most people find they are not tough enough or quick enough. Then they have a choice: They can work on their games and learn to compete against the big boys, or they can go back to their comfort zone.

Most go back to their comfort zone.

And that's okay—but not if you want to get to the next level.

Or, like my brother Kevin, they decide to pursue another goal. Kevin knew he would never be an outstanding basketball player, but he also knew he could run, and with time, effort, and hard work, that he could become a successful runner. He steered his ship in the choppy waters of elite running competitions for a long time—but he chose the sea he wanted to sail in and learned how to navigate in any conditions.

Let's take it a step farther. Say you are a college basketball player and you want to make it to the NBA. As a college basketball player you are already incredibly successful; after all, only a very small percentage of high school players even make it to the college level. Reaching the NBA is an even bigger step.

Why? NBA players are able to do things no one else on the planet can do. NBA players possess a remarkable combination of size, speed, power, leaping ability, athleticism, coordination...plus they run the floor while taking an absolute pounding...NBA players do things the average person cannot begin to imagine doing.

And that's just in practice.

If games are like battles, pro practices are like war. Most players work harder in practice than in games because they have to earn game time. Plus, pro players don't want to lose...at *anything*. They don't want to lose games, they don't want to lose in practice—basically they don't want to lose, at anything, each and every time they hit the court. At the pro level failure results in dramatic consequences, so players will do whatever it takes, and then some, to ensure they succeed.

So here's what I tell parents. If your child has what it takes to get off the elevator at the "need to be" floor, support them. In this case I don't mean "support" just in terms of encouragement; support means reinforcing the fact there are no shortcuts to success. No amount of spending, no amount of private coaching, and no amount of coddling will help your child reach the next level.

For example, send your child to a camp without his or her friends. Send them somewhere they won't be comfortable. Make it hard. Take them to play with the big boys. I was 5'2" as a freshman in high school. I went to a camp at Ohio University and played against seniors…and got the crap kicked out of me. The other players were bigger, stronger, faster, and more talented. They took no prisoners. I quickly realized what it would take to get to the next level. There will always be players who are quicker, stronger, and faster— *someone* will always be better than you. Your challenge is to face those players and determine how you can become better.

That's what competition is all about.

In a game everything won't go your way. You may face a hostile crowd, tight rims, or bad calls. You can't always change the conditions, but you can change the outcome.

The same is true in business. Facing competition and facing adversity will only make you better. Whether you choose to or are forced to steer the ship when the waters are anything but calm, learning how to steer the ship in choppy waters can improve your skills and open up new opportunities. Meet your challenges head on, communicate—and if there is an elephant in the room, discuss it and make it disappear.

Then you will earn the kind of gray hair you can be proud of.

And you will gain self-confidence that is based on real success, real achievement, and real results.

Thirteen

Self Confidence: Yes.
Ego: No

H ere is a definition of the word "ego" that I love:

Ego is a contagious disease that makes everyone in the room sick... except for the person who has it.

Or, from another perspective:

Ego is always individual: Players win individual awards and accolades.

Self-confidence is team-based and team-oriented: Teams win championships.

In 1973, when I was in college, the Cleveland Cavaliers held their training camp on our campus. During the camp the Cavaliers played the Detroit Pistons in a pre-season game, and I was asked to work the Pistons bench. Of course I jumped at the opportunity: If you want to be successful, watch and learn from what successful people do.

Even though it was only a pre-season game, both teams played hard and clearly wanted to win. In the third quarter, Al Attles, the Pistons coach, was ejected. (Yes, coaches even care a lot about pre-season games. Coaches, like players, want to win—all the time.)

At the time Bob Lanier, a six-time All Star, was the Pistons big man and Dave Bing, a seven-time All Star (and currently the Mayor of Detroit), was their star guard. During one time-out Bing took over the huddle. He said, "Here's all we have to do. You guys focus on defense. I'll take care of the offense."

That was it. That was the plan. They didn't set anything up, didn't talk about strategy, and didn't make contingency plans or try to adjust to what the Cavaliers were doing. Dave just said he would take over the offense. He relied on his teammates to play great defense.

They didn't win, but that's not the point.

Dave Bing was an All-Star and incredibly talented player. He was justifiably confident in his abilities. He was willing to put the team on his back. He wanted the ball. He possessed real self-confidence.

Not ego; self-confidence.

There's a huge difference. Early on in my professional career my boss said to me, "You act like this is your company."

I said "No, I don't feel that way at all. I'm just extremely committed. I am willing to work hard. I have always felt I should work as hard as I would if it was my company, but I know it's not."

He said, "That's fine, but why have you never introduced me as your boss?"

I have to admit I was momentarily speechless. I had never thought about what he was saying. I always introduced him by name, not title. To me, titles don't matter. People matter. Titles don't get jobs done. People get jobs done. In my mind he was above me on the organizational chart but still, like me, an important member of the team, just like the people below me on the organizational chart were also important members of the team.

So I said, "Okay, will do." From then on, I introduced him to everyone as my boss. He wanted people to know, so I let everyone know.

That's ego.

Sure, I followed instructions, but I thought it was silly. Business isn't the military. Leaders don't have to wear stripes on their uniforms so people know who they are. People know who you are by how you carry yourself.

And if people don't know your job title or position—who cares? Recognition is the last thing a good leader seeks. Leaders work for their employees. Leaders are like the keys to the car. Leaders provide the tools. *Teams* succeed. Leaders can succeed—but only as a member of a team.

Great leaders carry self-confidence wherever they go. Great leaders check their egos at the door.

Who is the greatest basketball player of all time? We can argue all day, but many people will say Michael Jordan is the greatest player of all time. For the sake of argument, let's assume he is. Michael Jordan, great as he was, could not and did not win championships on his own. For years Michael piled up incredible stats and an amazing collection of highlight reels. But only when he was surrounded by good players—and when he focused on helping make his teammates better—did the Bulls win six NBA championships.

No one person can win a game on their own. (But anyone can lose a game on their own, since a team is only as strong as its weakest link.)

Think back to the 1950s and 1960s. The greatest player, based on statistics alone, was Wilt Chamberlain. Some seasons he averaged over 25 rebounds a game; in fact, he once scored 100 points in a single game. During that same time period, Bill Russell's Celtics teams won ten NBA championships.

Individually Russell's statistics did not stack up to Wilt's.

So: Who was the greater player?

To me, Russell was the greater player. Wilt did eventually play on two championship teams—the Sixers and the Lakers—but his teams did not win it all until he had good players surrounding him and he learned to rely on his teammates as well as on his own skills and abilities.

Statistics are individual achievements; winning is a *team* achievement.

Here's one of my favorite quotes from the late, great John Wooden:

> *Talent was God-given; be humble. Fame is man-given;*
> *be grateful. Conceit is self-given; be careful.*

I spoke with Coach Wooden several times. He was an incredible man with absolutely no pretensions or ego in spite of the fact he was, in my opinion, the greatest college coach of all time. His response to a reporter sums up who he was as a person and how he approached working with and developing young men.

After Coach Wooden retired, a reporter said, "Coach, you've had a storied career. Who was the greatest player you coached?"

Coach Wooden replied, "That's a really good question. To answer it, we'll need to wait about twenty-five years to see what all those young men have become."

In business, self-confidence is based on knowing you have the right team supporting you. At Dynamic Drinkware, our sales reps are self-confident. They know as an organization we will come through because we have in the past, time after time after time after time. Our sales reps promise customers that quality product will be delivered on specific dates based on the knowledge our entire team can and will do what it takes to make it happen.

Having the right team behind you creates confidence. I am confident in my own abilities, but I am incredibly confident that with the help of our team I will come through on promises I make to our customers. On our team, we rely on each other. We need each other. We come through for each other. When times get tough, we stay confident because we know we're not alone—and we know we can and will come through.

That's why we have a little swagger in our steps. We have a strong belief in our abilities. As Dizzie Dean, the old-school Hall of Fame pitcher used to say, "It ain't braggin' if you done it." But confidence and swagger is based on team success. You can walk with confidence if you know the CEO is doing his or her job, the salespeople are selling, the quality department ensures the best product possible, the engineers are designing and developing, production is meeting targets…you feel confident because the team you represent is strong.

Sometimes that lesson takes a while to learn. Years ago a friend of mine was the V.P. of Sales for a major corporation and was promoted to President. He asked me to come out for a visit. I congratulated him on earning his new position, and we talked about the fact he was looking for a V.P. of Sales to take his place.

I said, "I didn't realize you were still looking to fill that role—it's been open for more than five weeks."

He paused, and said, "Yeah, I know. I thought I could do both jobs myself, but I've realized I can't. Would you like to take on the job?" For a time his ego led him to believe he was capable of filling both positions, but to his credit he quickly realized doing both jobs was impossible—impossible for anyone, not just for him.

We talked further, and I realized he was offering me a great opportunity, but I still asked one more question. "Are you going to turn over the keys to the Vice President's office? If not, give me your keys to the President's office."

He laughed, and so did I, but at the same time I was serious. He couldn't do both jobs, obviously. I couldn't either. But he did have to be willing to let me run with my ball. We needed each other, we needed people around us—and we had to be willing to turn everyone in the organization loose to run with their individual balls so the team could succeed. It's easy to assume you can do a job better than some other person. Whether or not that is in fact true is irrelevant: Your goal is to help that person be the best they can be—team success is the only outcome that matters.

Want an early warning signal of the onset of the ego disease? If you catch yourself using the pronoun "I," the ego virus may have entered your system. "I" didn't land a new customer. "I" didn't get a shipment out on time. "I" didn't develop a new product.

"We" did—because no one does anything worthwhile on their own.

Individual accomplishments are only important if those accomplishments support and promote team goals. If you aren't confident in your team, you either haven't done enough to help your team do a better job or you have the wrong people in the wrong places.

If you think you are the most important member of your team, your ego has gotten out of hand. Take a step back.

Knowing the difference between ego and self-confidence can make or break you as a leader.

Ego is destructive; self-confidence is a by-product of *team*, not *individual*, success.

Check your ego at the door. Develop self-confidence—in yourself and in your team members—by working *together* to achieve success.

Fourteen

Never Underestimate
Your Opponent

W hen I was playing, I loved to watch opposing teams
warm up. Sometimes what I saw was a confidence
booster, but mostly I looked for indications of what individual players might do during the game.

I watched everything. If a player opened a door with
his right hand, I knew he was right-handed. If one used his
left hand at the water fountain, I knew he was left-handed.
Sometimes what players do in warm-ups is misleading,
because some will intentionally use their less dominant hand
more frequently since that's where they feel they need the
most preparation. Some people, in sports and in business,

are smart enough to focus on improving their weaknesses instead of simply doing what comes more naturally.

So warm-up drills could be misleading—but water fountains never were.

I also checked body types. If a player had thin ankles, thick hamstrings, and a large butt...I knew I would probably have my hands full.

I scout people in business, too. I watch out for people who are composed, focused, and competitive (a tricky balance to maintain; lots of competitive people struggle to stay focused and composed, especially when conversations or negotiations get contentious.) I also look at shoes; if a person's shoes are scuffed, that says a lot. (Unless the people with scuffed shoes are managers who spend a lot of time on the shop floor; in that case I can tell they spend time in the trenches where they belong.)

Of course quick evaluations can at times be inaccurate, but small indicators tend to be accurate more often than not. I especially look for people who appear to bite their nails. I love to compete with nervous people—I do my best to stress them out and make it even harder for them to perform at their best.

After all, isn't that what competition boils down to? As a player my goal is to take an opponent away from what he wants to do and force him to do things he doesn't want to do. If I can play my game while taking you out of your game—I'll win.

Always scout your opponents carefully, but never judge and never assume—your opponents may be better than you think. As a friend of mine liked to say, "Never trust the fat man at a dance—they're smooth." The same premise is also true at the other end of the spectrum: If you compete against a champion, he or she will do whatever they need to do to win. (That's why they're champions.)

And never think you are better than everyone, no matter how successful you may feel. Someone, somewhere, can and will beat you—even a person who appears to be less successful. Sometimes styles make all the difference. Take Mohammad Ali, one of the greatest fighters of all time. Ali knocked out Sonny Liston, knocked out George Foreman, and defeated Joe Frazier twice...but he struggled against Ken Norton, an otherwise inferior fighter. Ali lost the first fight when Norton broke Ali's jaw in the first round, won a split decision in the second fight, and lost a split decision the third time he fought Norton.

Ken Norton never beat another top-ranked opponent, but he gave Ali fits because his style worked against Ali. Ali was able to adapt his style to suit most opponents, but not Ken Norton.

That's no knock on Ken Norton. He was an outstanding fighter. But he was a fighter most people—including Ali himself, at least at first—assumed would be an easy win for Ali.

By the way: A former employee of mine, Scott LeDoux (the "Fighting Frenchman") was a professional boxer and fought Ali, Frazier, Foreman, Larry Holmes, Leon Spinks, Ken Norton...he fought the best heavyweights of the 1970s and early '80s. He said, bar none, the hardest puncher he ever fought was George Foreman. (He later went fifteen rounds with Ken Norton and lost by split decision; many people feel Scott won that fight.)

I once played golf with Scott and Jesse Venture, professional wrestler and later governor of Minnesota. The first time I met Jesse I was playing golf with Scott in Minneapolis. Scott asked if his friend could play with us, and I said sure. Up walks a guy with a pony tail, huge arms, and a larger than life personality...but at the time I didn't know who he was.

Scott teed off first, playing barefoot. He pulled his first drive left, about 225 yards down the fairway.

Jesse teed off next and drove the ball about 220 yards, right down the middle of the fairway. He was very happy with himself, hollering, "Hey, Scottie—look how far I hit that!"

Two drives in and I had already sized up the competition. I thought, "Oh, good; I'm going to have some fun today."

I teed off and flew my ball over Jesse's and into the middle of the fairway. I am relatively short and was a couple shirt sizes removed from a professional wrestler, but as I walked by Jesse I said, "You know, I gotta tell you. For a big guy, you hit like shit."

So, as I expected, one thing led to another and we agreed to play for money. Jesse knew nothing about me—to him I was just some business guy.

I took their money. They underestimated me.

In their own fashion they scouted me, but in a haphazard, unfocused way. But that does not mean everyone will do a poor job of scouting you. You can easily give a lot away, even if you don't intend to.

I remember a flight from Minneapolis to Chicago on Northwest Airlines. I was in first class. (I try to sit in first class whenever possible because that's where business travelers tend to sit and it's a great way to network and make connections.) I was sitting in my seat minding my own business and the guys in front of me were talking loudly. I couldn't help but overhear the conversation. In fact, I think the folks in the back of the plane could hear them. I tried not to listen, but then I realized they worked for FedEx and were (at that time) direct competitors of ours.

And they were talking business.

In ten minutes I learned everything I needed to know about their sales strategies, about which customers they targeted, about their value propositions, about their pricing schemes... they gave me all the ammunition I needed to beat them. They provided me with a complete scouting report on their own company as well as their specific customer strategies.

The same thing once happened on an elevator. A salesman was complaining about the company he had just made a presentation to. Maybe he felt better for getting things off his chest, but he also gave me information I could put to good use. I didn't have to dig or do any research at all—he gave everything away.

Your business is *your* business—keep it to yourself. Don't talk business on elevators, in lobbies, on planes... save your business conversations for private places. Let other people underestimate you and your company. In most cases the competition will be happy to underestimate you, especially if you as an individual and as a company do not constantly blow your own horn.

It's especially easy to underestimate your competition when you are successful. It's great to win championships. Sure, you work hard to reach the top—but you will have to work harder to stay there. Once you're at the top other teams will be gunning for you.

Recently I was speaking with a men's basketball staff member from a very successful team from the Big 12 Conference. This team ended the 2009–2010 season ranked in the top ten, losing in the Elite Eight of the NCAA tournament.

"Now when we play an unranked team, it's like their Final Four game. They wait for us. We're circled on their calendars. They want to take us down. We are the best team they will play all year, so they make the game an event. When we play in their arena it is absolute bedlam."

When you're a winner, all eyes are on you. You may be expected to win, and you may expect to win…but for the other team this game is their Super Bowl—not yours.

They won't underestimate you. They know exactly who you are. But you may underestimate them. I know. I've underestimated people.

For years I went to the Super Show, the largest sports trade show in the world. It was a lot of fun. One gentleman marketed a device to help people shoot free-throws, and I would often get challenged by kids. I would let the kids go first; if he made 24 in a row, I would make 25 and stop.

I never lost. (Remember, I've made the shot thousands and thousands of times.)

One year—the last year I attended, coincidentally—a friend of mine, Dennis Green, came down from Denver to attend the Show. He was wearing a sport coat, he was older than me...and then he challenged me to shoot. I wasn't worried or concerned. In fact, I didn't even want to shoot against him, but he insisted.

I didn't warm up. I assumed I would quickly put him away.

He beat me two straight times. He hit 38 straight, something I could do in my sleep...but I didn't.

Then he beat me again.

I felt like Mohammed Ali when he lost to Leon Spinks.

What happened? After all, I had only lost a few free-throw competitions in my entire life. But I wasn't ready to play. I hadn't warmed up, hadn't taken any shots, wasn't mentally focused and was, in short, overconfident. So he beat me—twice.

I was his Super Bowl; he wasn't mine.

When you're a champion, you have to work even harder to stay on top.

In business, you have to work harder to keep a job than you did to get the promotion. Expect to work harder when you're in the position—because other people, other companies, and even other employees are gunning for your spot.

Dennis, wherever you are: Call me. Let's shoot again.

I won't underestimate you this time.

Fifteen

Champions Are Made, Not Born

About five years ago USA Today published a fascinating article that attempted to answer a simple question: What is the Soul of a Champion?

Or put another way, what makes a champion a champion? Physical attributes? Winning the genetic lottery? Or is a champion the product of exceptional parenting or coaching?

While all of the above certainly helps, it turns out championship-caliber athletes like Michael Jordan, Roger Federer, Michael Phelps, Tom Brady, the Williams sisters, and Derek Jeter (to name just a few) all share four basic characteristics:

- **Competitiveness.** Champions thrive on the heat of battle. They love competition, and they want to have the ball at the end of the game. Pure and simple, they like to compete. (At just about anything—not just their particular sport.)

- **Confidence.** Individual-sport athletes are confident in themselves and in the team behind them: Their coaches, trainers, advisors, etc. Team-sport athletes have a swagger based on knowing the guys and girls behind them have their backs.

- **Composure.** Champions stay calm and focused even when everything around them is crumbling. Think about Michael Jordan: How many game-winning shots did he make? A lot…but he missed a lot more. Champions don't linger on mistakes and don't let past errors affect them. At crunch time, champions can stay under control emotionally and still perform well.

- **Focus.** Champions don't worry about yesterday or tomorrow. They exhibit a laser-like focus on the present—on what needs to be done *right now*.

Now ask yourself why the same companies always seem to get the big orders. Ask yourself why the same sales reps tend to make the big sales. They are competitive, they are confident, they stay calm and composed, and they focus on taking care of business. Put another way, those companies have a plan, an organization, a system…and they play within that system.

They have built winning traditions.

Success breeds success...and more success.

The championship difference lies in the gap between talent and hard work. Lots of people are talented. Talented athletes come along all the time. Think back to when you were in school; odds are some of the best athletes in 6th, 7th, or 8th grade did not turn out to be the best athletes in high school. Success came early and those individuals did not try to improve. Over time other kids caught up—and passed them.

In fact, the worst combination a coach can receive is a player who is athletic but not skilled. Raw athleticism can overcome a lack of skill, at least for awhile. Eventually, at higher levels, skill will overcome raw athleticism. Natural ability is no longer enough. At the top levels of sport, players are athletic *and* skilled. At the top levels of business, successful people are talented *and* skilled; they leverage their natural abilities by constantly working at their trades.

How do you translate the Soul of a Champion to the work environment? Let's start with a person just entering the workforce. Say you just graduated from college and have landed your first job.

While you received an education, your education has in fact just begun.

The key is to surround yourself with other people who are successful. Start by finding someone in the organization that is successful; spend as much time observing that person for a week. Reinventing the "performance" wheel makes no sense; all you have to do is mimic the successful person's traits and work habits. Then, after a week or so you will have a sense of which people in the organization are not particularly successful; spend as much time as you can observing those people the second week.

Then *don't* do what they do.

Learn what to do from successful people. Learn what not to do from unsuccessful people. It really is that simple. Don't start out trying to do things "your way." You don't know enough about the company or the industry to really know what works and what doesn't work. Why use trial and error when great examples exist all around you?

What you'll probably find is the person who is successful gets to the office early, talks to customers, joins teams, helps others, does things outside the office to improve his or her skills . . . while the unsuccessful person gets to work just in the nick of time, leaves right on time, and has to manage her co-ed softball team on Thursdays, no matter what.

You'll find the keys to success are fairly simple.

The same approach applies to sports. Pick a successful player and study his or her moves. Watch the way they rebound and emulate what they do. All you have to do in order to succeed is to watch what successful people do—as long as you work at what you learn and put it into practice, you can be successful, too.

Here's the key. Most people talk about adding years to their lives, and that's great . . . but at the same time, why not add life to your years? Experience can be gained quickly or slowly—it's up to you. Measure your experience in terms of hours, not days.

The best way to add life to your years is to stay busy. You can rest when you die.

Champions don't rest—why do you think you should be any different?

Think in terms of focus. Champions are incredibly focused. I don't know him, but I feel sure Roger Federer thinks about tennis most of the time. If you want to succeed in business, business should be your focus. Say you like to read: I like Nelson DeMille novels as much as the next person, but if you're in the business world, very few people will ask if you've read the latest DeMille mystery. Reading novels simply will not help you in your chosen field. Instead, read business books, motivational books, trade journals... focus your reading on subjects that will help you succeed. Entertainment is, well, entertaining... but it won't help you succeed.

A couple of years ago I spoke at a corporate convention in North Carolina. North Carolina is a Mecca of basketball, and naturally people asked me who I thought would win the upcoming NCAA Tournament.

Sports are fun. Watching sports is fun. Talking about sports is fun.

But are sports important?

Not really.

For my own amusement I asked the 200 people at the conference if they could tell me the names of the four teams that made it to the Final Four the previous year.

They couldn't. Remember, I was in Carolina, the home of North Carolina, North Carolina State, Wake Forest, and Duke. Talk about basketball country!

So I asked if they knew who won the World Series two years ago.

They didn't.

I asked if they could tell me who won the AFC Championship three years ago.

They couldn't.

They didn't remember because sports are entertaining, but sports are not important.

What *is* important? What matters most to me are family, spirituality, health, and my family's financial well-being.

All we take with us when we die is our good name and our morals. That is all anyone will remember about any of us. Everything else is temporary. So why not play hard, play to win, try to be successful—and focus on what is important?

When you start to move up the organization and assume your first leadership position, your education continues. Say you are a first-time leader; what should you do?

Assemble your team, make sure they understand team and the organization goals, make sure everyone pulls in the same direction, and make sure everyone is on the bus.

Don't try to make huge changes or to prove yourself, at least not right away. You don't have to immediately show that you're the man. What you do have to show is respect for all the individuals on your team. Good managers look at their team, look at each person's capabilities, and make sure the right people are in the right places.

Your job is to guide and direct your team and find ways to help them succeed.

Again, you work for your employees; they don't work for you.

Then, when you do make changes, make sure you know what you are changing *from,* and more importantly what you will change *to.* What is the short-term effect of the change? What are the long-term effects of the change? Team attitude determines altitude; if you make too many changes too quickly, some employees will put more energy into complaining instead of reaching for higher altitudes. Keep your door open, consider and discuss new ideas, and ensure everything you and your employees do supports and promotes both team and organization-wide goals.

Most importantly, understand you cannot be your employees' friend. That's why head coaches have assistants. Assistants can be like friends to players, but the head coach has to have respect and maintain a certain amount of distance from his or her players.

Finally, look the part, act the part, and make leading your team a full-time effort. If you can't, be honest with yourself and your employer. Commit to doing whatever it takes—if you aren't willing, don't take the job. If you aren't willing to work for your employees, don't take the job.

Your boss may not feel the same way about how he approaches his or her job, of course. Many bosses feel their employees work for them, leaving their employees feeling stifled, unsupported, and lacking mentoring and advice and guidance.

If you have a bad boss, what can you do?

I've been in that position several times, sadly. But I have learned what not to do from bad bosses, so in that sense the experience was not wasted.

Let's look at two different scenarios. In the first scenario, have faith that cream will always rise to the top. Companies don't change, but people do. If you feel your boss is a bad boss, other people do as well...and eventually upper management will figure things out and will make the changes necessary. Be patient, do your work, bide your time, work hard to improve your skills...and stick it out.

But in the meantime, don't talk to other employees about the situation. Don't bad-mouth your boss. Complaining to other employees will always come back to bite you.

Also keep in mind you may have to leave the company. In the second scenario, when a company is family owned or family-operated and your boss is related to the owners...changes are unlikely to be made, regardless of how well or how poorly your boss performs. In that case you may have to find another job.

I can count on one hand the number of times I've heard about a father firing his son or daughter, or a sister firing her brother. It just doesn't happen.

America is the greatest free enterprise system in the world. You can accomplish anything you have the skills and drive to accomplish. You can do anything. The downside is that anyone can do anything...and if the guy "doing it" in your company is not only a bad boss but also owns the company, you may have to elect not to play on his team any longer.

That happened to me: I relocated to what appeared to be a great company but my boss was the owner's son. I always assume I will outwork, outhustle, and outlast bad bosses and rise to the top...but I realized that would never happen in this case. The son would never leave—or be asked to leave—the company, and there was no road left for me to travel. I took my time, was patient, and made sure I knew what I was changing to before I made a change...but eventually I left for another position with another company.

Bad boss or not, keep in mind your biggest fight should always be with someone on the street, not with someone inside your own building. You don't have to agree with every decision, but once a decision is made, you must go forward with that decision and support it. Otherwise you need to leave.

Once I had a boss who often said, "We can disagree as much as we like in this room, but after we make a decision, we all must leave the room and fully support that decision—even if you disagreed in private. We are all one team and we all walk together."

In short, if you are not in agreement with a decision, you should still always root for your team to succeed. In basketball, when you hit the court you must do everything you can to help each other. You don't have to be friends off the court but all five players must play together on the court.

Sometimes your boss may not be as "bad" as you think. Everyone doesn't get along with their boss. If you are in that situation, there are two sides to every coin. What you feel might be real, but your boss probably has less than positive feelings about you, too.

Are you part of the problem? If you are the only employee with a problem, the common denominator in that problem is you. (It takes maturity to recognize and admit we are part of the problem.)

Again, are you part of the problem? Why not find out? Ask. Let's say you realize you and your boss aren't on the same wavelength. Ask what you can do to improve the relationship. You may find out your boss actually likes you and respects your performance. Or you may not—either way, you will have opened the lines of communication.

Just remember that a good boss, like a good basketball coach, has one primary focus: Getting the most out of his or her team with the talent available. Sometimes a coach may have to motivate players, kick them in the butt, point them in the right direction, tell the truth, and recognize success and failure, no matter how uncomfortable that might be for the player or the coach. The same is true in business.

And never forget to know the history of what you do. Know the industry, know the changes, know the players, and make decisions based on knowledge, not on hunches or whims.

What makes a champion? Champions are competitive, confidence, composed, and focused.

What is your focus? Do you hope to get rich? I hope you do—but in a different way than you might think. My definition of "rich" is not what you take up; but what you give up makes you rich. We all work for two things: To make money and to have fun. Find a balance between the two that makes you happy. You may have to give up some amount of wealth in order to be happy; you may have to give up some degree of happiness in order to build wealth.

Focus on what makes you happy—and go get it. Happiness is the true definition of success.

That's the Soul of a Champion.

Sixteen

Mission Statements

I did not agree with everything my mother and father said when I was young. (I was a teenager, after all, and like most teenagers thought I knew more than I really did.) But over the years I came to understand just how smart my parents really were and how much I benefited from their wisdom, experience, and guidance.

But in one instance at least, I still feel they were wrong.

My parents—along with millions of other people, I'm sure—used to say, "When my ship comes in...." The implication was that someday, somehow, circumstances would be in their favor and things would "work out." Their ship would come in. Your ship would come in. My ship would come in.

Wrong: Ships don't come to us. Our ships may exist—but they are out there waiting for us. We must actively look for opportunities. We must make things happen. Fate won't do it for us. Circumstances won't align "someday."

Besides, why wonder if and when your ship will come in? Never assume opportunities will come looking for you because in my experience, they don't. You can't control what other people do. You can't control circumstances. You can't control which doors open for you.

But you can control what you do. Decide what you want to do and decide who you want to be. Determine your dreams and your goals and swim out to them.

Here's my personal mission statement:

Do not wait for your ship to come in—swim out to it.

That's it. That's my mission statement. I live by it.

Mission statements are important. Mission statements set direction. Too many people start a job or become a member of a team without knowing their role. Too many people don't know what is expected of them. They know their job title, sure—but what does a job title really mean?

I heard one of my favorite sayings at one of our customer's national meetings. The company hired ASE Group, a firm specializing in delivering presentations for large corporate groups. The owner of the company, Bonnie Siegel, said, "As the story goes, if you give a man a fish he eats for a day. If you teach a man to fish, he eats for a lifetime." It's a simple statement, but it's memorable and cuts right to the point.

In basketball I may be a point guard, but "point guard" means different things in different offensive schemes and to different teams. On some teams, my job as a point guard may be to bring the ball up the floor, run the offense, make great passes, and get back on defense. How many points I score may be secondary; in fact, on some teams point guards by design only score a handful of points a game. Their main focus is to set up scoring opportunities for teammates. In that case, a point guard who scores a lot is actually not doing his job.

On other teams, the point guard may be expected to score more. Individual expectations are based on team needs and team goals.

In short, "point guard" describes a *position* but not necessarily a *role*. A mission statement helps every player—or member of a corporate team—understand his or her role.

Most of the time mission statements take time to establish. If you start a new company it should take six months to a year to really figure out how to run the company. You may have ideas about how you will bring products to market, for example, but I can almost guarantee what you *think* you will do will turn out to be different than what you *actually* do. No matter how much time and effort goes into creating a comprehensive business plan, you will have to adapt and adjust to market forces, competition, changes in the economy—you'll have to make adjustments based on how the "game" plays out.

Plus, in many ways a business plan is naturally reactive. Business plans are based on evaluating current conditions and developing strategies to take advantage of those conditions. Think about one of the major components of the typical business plan: A competitive analysis. A competitive analysis is based on current market conditions (with some predictions and a few guesses thrown in for good measure) and shows how, hopefully, your company can successfully compete with other companies in the space.

A competitive analysis in a business plan is reactive; no matter how hard you try to predict the future, the bulk of the analysis is based on competing with the business players who are currently on the floor.

Later, you will become proactive as you better understand your competition, your market, and your customers. Then you'll know what kind of company you are—and you can develop a meaningful mission statement.

We took a fair amount of time to develop our mission statement at Dynamic Drinkware. We knew ships were out there…we just weren't sure which ships we should swim to. We knew people needed cups. We knew that while all cups at a basic level hold liquid, ours looked better. We felt sure—but we didn't *know*—if consumers would pay more for a cup that looks better. We knew we could make beautiful cups. Through testing and market research we knew consumers preferred our cups. But would they pay more for them?

Convincing concessionaires to purchase our cups was just one step in the process. End consumers were and are the ultimate judge of our success. We can sell to our customers, the concessionaires and retailers…but the end consumer has to appreciate and buy the product from those retailers or all our efforts are in vain. Without consumer acceptance we have no business.

So we started with a rough idea of our mission. We knew we had major advantages on our side, then and now. Our cups are made in the U.S. We have a highly skilled workforce and outstanding engineers. We manufacture product using equipment we have developed and modified specifically for our purposes. We knew what we had going for us: A skilled workforce, using modern technology, providing second-to-none customer service, delivering an exponentially better-looking cup.

That's where we started.

Keep in mind customers do not care about mission statements. In fact, customers should not care about mission statements. Customers care about what you *deliver.* Customers care about your products, your services, the value they receive...plus intangibles like outstanding customer service. That's what you deliver. What you deliver is the proof of your mission statement. Our customers know that if they buy our cups they will sell, on average, approximately 30% more beverages. Consumers love our cups. Consumers buy our cups. The ultimate judge—the consumer—loves what we do. As a result, our customers do, too.

Employees care about mission statements. Customers don't. So don't advertise your mission statement outside your company. No one cares. Customers won't buy from you based on a mission statement. They *will* buy from you based on the value you provide.

Mission statements should, therefore, be simple. A relatively long mission statement means either you are trying to do too many things or you haven't really thought about what you seek to accomplish. What type of company are you? Do you focus on efficient manufacturing in order to be the lowest-cost provider? Do you focus on service? Do you focus on quality?

Take automakers: While they both make cars, Mercedes adopts a much different approach than, say, Hyundai. Mercedes sells quality; Hyundai sells value.

Take consumer electronics: Apple sells the "wow" factor by constantly redefining what customers expect, focusing less on price and more on innovation. Vizio, a flat-panel TV manufacturer, has become a leader in its field by seeking to be a low-cost provider. Innovation is important, but delivering at a low price point is everything to a company like Vizio.

Regardless of your direction, your employees must know and buy into your mission statement.

Even basketball teams have mission statements, whether spoken or implied. A basketball team's mission statement can be summed up with a visual. Five players are on the floor at a time. When all five play as a team, those five people make a fist. Fists are powerful and strong. Stick one finger out and it's easy to break off. Pull together as a team and each individual benefits from the strength of his teammates. When one player goes in a different direction and a finger sticks out from the fist, not only is that player weaker and easier to "break off" but the entire team becomes weaker.

If you are a member of a team and you don't know where to go...shame on your manager. (For fun, ask your employees to write down your company mission statement. If they don't know it, they should.)

If you are a member of a team and you know the mission statement, you know the direction, you know the goals, you know your role, but you don't agree with the mission...shame on you. If you can't bring effort, emotion and enthusiasm on a daily basis, get out. Do something else. You owe it to yourself and to your company. Find a job where you can give your best, unreservedly. (Just make sure you fully understand what you are changing from and what you will be changing to.)

Do two things, right now. One, develop a mission statement for your company or your team. If you have one, make sure everyone understands and embraces that mission. Know where you're going.

Two, and just as important, develop your personal mission statement. You don't have to reinvent the wheel. If you want to borrow mine, feel free; it's served me well.

Don't wait for your ship to come in—swim out to it.

Seventeen

The Future of Our Youth

We live in a society of instant gratification. People want things now. Not later. Not tomorrow. Not next year.

Now.

The average young person today wants to get to the final destination without making the trip. They think they're ready.

Partly that feeling is due to technology. Communication now is almost instantaneous. In the "old days" we had to wait to communicate: Wait until we got home to make a phone call, wait for tomorrow's paper to find out how the stock market performed, wait for the mail to arrive to find out how our relatives were doing . . . today we can know almost anything we want to know within moments. That's a good thing. But instantaneous communication has created a shift in expectations.

A much greater factor, frankly, is a shift in how we parent our children. We ease our kids through things. We enable them. We help them. You can't blame us: We all want the best for our kids. So we do whatever we can to ensure our kids achieve the things they want to achieve: We pay for private coaching, private tutors, expensive camps…we argue with teachers and administrators about how our kids are treated…we are all "mama bears" and "papa bears" where our kids are concerned. Is it possible we love our kids too much?

The problem is—and I think it's a major problem—by doing so we deny our kids the opportunity to make the trip. What makes you successful at the end of any trip is what you learn along the way. The journey is everything. Education and experience cannot be purchased; they must be earned. In business, I look for people who have made the trip. I look for people who have worked hard and paid their dues. I look for people who learned from their experiences. I look for people with gray hair, whether symbolic or actual.

I surround myself with people who have made the journey. Then I know we'll reach our destination. What we've learned along the way makes us who we are. Our experiences create wisdom, knowledge, and judgment. In life, the journey truly is everything.

I wouldn't trade my journey for anything. I graduated from college in 1976. During my senior year I coached a youth basketball team. One of the parents was a big supporter of the team and provided financial assistance so we could attend a tournament in another city. He and I spent a fair amount of time together and he got to know me. I guess he liked what he saw because he hired me to work for his company, part-time, during my last semester of school.

The industry I worked in isn't important; what matters is I traveled to conferences and trade shows, worked booths, talked to people, and began to develop sales skills. It was my first "real" job since I had worked in our family ice cream store. I got to see a lot of different places when we traveled, which broadened my horizons. I realized I wanted to do more than just coach. I enjoyed education and loved working with kids, but I knew I wanted to do more. Traveling with his company opened my eyes to a wider range of possibilities.

Yet there I was, in Cleveland (a city at the time teetering on the brink of bankruptcy), suffering through cold winters, not sure where opportunities would come from...so I decided to move. I couldn't afford to move to Phoenix, a city I loved, couldn't afford to live in New York, another city I loved...so after some thought decided moving to Columbus, Ohio would be relatively affordable and fun.

I graduated from college on June 11. On June 13 I loaded all my possessions in my car, drove to Columbus, and checked into the Holiday Inn on the west side of town.

I had no job. In fact, I didn't know a soul who lived in Columbus. But like a high school athlete hoping to be recruited by a college coach, all I wanted was to find an opportunity. I just needed someone to leave a little crack in a door so I could push through.

I hit the streets hard and it only took me a couple days to land a job with Continental Insurance, at that time one of the largest insurance companies in the United States. As a new hire, I entered their sixteen-week management training program. The program was intense and so was the anticipation. Continental Insurance committed to training us; we, in return, agreed to be placed anywhere in the country, in any department, that Continental wished once our training was complete. So as you can guess a fair amount of jockeying and positioning went on; some people were fine with the idea of moving to another city, while others were less excited by the prospect. Others wanted to work in specific departments. In a way the training period was like an audition and we were all competing for roles.

As it turned out, they must have liked me. Instead of shipping me off to God knows where, they kept me at the Columbus headquarters. I found a room to rent and started to put down roots, such as they were. After work I played ball—old habits die hard—and went to a local church, talked to the Christian Youth Organization folks, and asked if they needed a coach. They hired me and we won the city championship several years in a row. At some point in my tenure as coach a gentleman approached me and asked if he could be my assistant. He loved basketball, loved kids, and had previously asked the organization if he could help, but without success.

I agreed, but under one condition. "Show up on time, show up every time, do things my way...and we'll be fine," I said.

To his credit, he did.

He also ran a corporation that included an advertising agency. Midway through the first season he asked me to work for him in sales. I was working a desk job with Continental; I liked the company and liked the work, to a degree, but was excited by the challenge of getting out of the office and working directly with customers. So I took the job.

I loved it. In fact, I loved it so much I eventually purchased the advertising portion of the business from him, and that's how I landed my Fortune 500 job with Purolator Courier. I signed Purolator as a customer, did a great job for them, and they ended up hiring me away from my own company.

They didn't have a current opening, so they created one for me. Purolator put together a development plan that moved me from position to position, step by step, and I became the Director of National Sales after a little less than three years.

Was it hard to leave my own business and take a corporate job working for someone else? Not really: I saw an opportunity to gain more experience and to work in different parts of the country. I called on every Fortune 500 company east of the Rocky Mountains, and once delivered a presentation to Lee Iacocca, then the head of Chrysler and justly famous for turning the company around during its darkest hours.

Purolator made a lot of promises, and they came through on those promises. While I could not know for sure whether they would deliver on my development plan, I wasn't worried. I was confident I could make mid-game adjustments no matter what happened. Even if they had not made me Director of National Sales, I knew I would learn a ton.

I knew the journey would be worth it, even if the destination turned out to be different than I expected.

Today we focus on getting our kids to the destination when we should focus on helping them learn from the journey. My father earned enough money to send us to college, but he took a different approach: He decided we would benefit greatly from working at the ice cream store and putting aside the money we earned for college. Sure, we benefited financially, but I gained more in skills and experience than I earned in dollars: I learned how to show up every day, on time, and take pride in my work. I learned responsibility. I learned how to treat customers. I learned how to prioritize, how to manage my time, how to manage money, how to be responsible...in short, I learned how to delay gratification.

I had big dreams, and the journeys I took helped me understand dreams don't come true overnight—but they do come true if you put in the work. I learned reaching my dreams was like constructing a large building: No matter how big it may turn out to be, you still build a building one brick at a time. I also learned you can destroy a large building, even one that took years to build, with just one swing of a bat. The same holds true in relationships: It may take years to build a relationship, yet you can destroy one in seconds.

The journey is everything. We don't do our kids a favor when we make their success easy. We don't do our kids a favor when we pull strings, use our influence, or throw money at a problem or opportunity in order to achieve a desired outcome. When you throw money at a goal you may reach the destination ... but you also skip the journey. When your kid gets in trouble at school and you talk the principal out of taking disciplinary action, you deny your child the opportunity to learn from a journey—even if that journey is momentarily unpleasant.

When my friend and I started to paint the wrong house, I have no doubt my father could have gotten me out of it. But he didn't. In fact, my dad did not even know about the problem. Asking my father to "save" me was never an option. We made a mistake and we made it right. Was correcting our mistake and making things right momentarily unpleasant? Absolutely. But I learned a life lesson by seeing my mistake through. The journey mattered. The end result did not.

We owe it to young people to help create those journeys. In fact, they *want* us to create those journeys. Kids want to be like us. They naturally seek role models. When I was young, my older brother Jim was nine years older than me. He was an outstanding runner; he held his high school record in the 800 meters and the mile. Jim and his friends were athletes. I wanted to be like them. I wanted to hang out with them.

They didn't let me. I wasn't accepted because I was too young. Plus, I had a quick tongue and a big mouth so his friends really did not want me around. Years later I learned that his friend Tom had plotted to ease his pain by having me disappear forever. Yes, he was going to have me exterminated. (Ouch!)

I learned—even at a young age—that just because someone is younger doesn't mean you can't make a difference in their lives...even if you are young yourself. The Little League team that goes to McDonald's after a game, still wearing their uniforms, is a role model for other kids. Every younger kid in the restaurant wants to be like them. Every kid wants to wear that uniform. Every kid wants to be part of a team.

When I got older I coached my younger brother Patrick's basketball team. I took the job partly because I love basketball, and even then I loved working with children, but mainly I coached his team because I had not felt accepted when I was that age. I learned from my experiences and decided to do things differently when it was my turn. That's why I've coached so many teams, at all different levels of sport.

Today, it's incredibly gratifying when someone approaches me, most often after a speech, and asks if I remember them. Recently I was in Columbus and needed to rent a truck. The clerk looked at me a couple times, and said, "Are you still making behind-your-back half-court shots?"

It turns out I had coached him twenty-five years ago. We had a nice chat, and it felt awesome that, in some small way, I had made an impression and a difference in his life.

My college coach was Don Delaney, better known to many as "Double D." Coach Delaney was the perfect college coach; he was highly intense and expected 100% perfection from each and every player. Yet Coach Delaney was also very close to each of us. To a man we had the utmost respect for Double D, as a coach and as a person. Coach taught me that I was not small... just not very tall. He inspired me to be tough and gave me the opportunities I was looking for.

At the end of my last season we finished with a record of 27–4. More importantly, as teammates we truly cared for each other. Coach Delaney is quite a guy—on and off the floor. He had a very successful coaching career, later becoming the head coach of the Cleveland Cavaliers. Like most of my other coaches, he helped me become a better player.

To the world you might be just one person, but to one person you just might be the world.

The difference you make is everything. I looked up to my brother and his friends. I wanted to be like them. Today I try to model myself after people I admire. (Why reinvent the wheel?) Eighty year-olds can be role models. Ten year-olds can be role models.

Ten year-olds can benefit from the journey. The destination doesn't matter. The journey is everything.

Help the people around you benefit from the journey. You can do whatever you want to do. The word "American" ends in "I can."

You, and your children, can do whatever you want to do and can reach any destination you desire—the journeys you take make success possible.

You owe it to the youth today to help provide those journeys.

Don't enable the _destination_.

Enable the _journey_.

Eighteen

750 Is a Nice Round Number

Whether is the easiest shot in basketball?

If you said a layup is the easiest shot, you are not alone. Most people think a layup is the easiest shot. (Granted, a dunk is arguably the easiest shot...but most of us can't jump that high, so dunking is a moot point.)

Close your eyes and imagine: Final seconds of a game, the score is tied, you have the ball and are driving to the basket...but the opposing team's center quickly rotates over...and he'll do anything he can to stop you. Suddenly you have a lot of decisions to make: Should you go right, go left, duck under, use a head fake and pull up for a short jumper...no matter what you decide, at that moment you are in a fight for your basketball life.

Trust me: A layup is not the easiest shot in basketball. The easiest shot is a completely uncontested shot: A free-throw. Every time you shoot a free-throw you can follow the same routine, use the same fundamentals, and shoot the ball exactly the same way...with no one guarding you.

The only real pressure you face when you shoot a free-throw is you are required to shoot within ten seconds of receiving the ball...but then again, how often do you see that particular rule enforced? Realistically, all you have to do is make the shot.

A free-throw is the easiest shot in basketball because it is what it sounds like: A free-throw is *free*. Making a free-throw is simply a matter of understanding basic fundamentals, executing those fundamentals...and putting in lots and lots of practice.

A free-throw, in short, is like a microcosm of the business world: No matter what your industry, you decide what you want to do, you determine the best way to do what you want to do, and you practice so you can execute what you want to do, successfully, reliably, time after time. Learning to shoot the perfect free-throw is no different than determining the best way to manufacture a product, take an order, or complete an inspection.

Even if you have played basketball for most of your life, you are probably at best a mediocre free-throw shooter. Or, you may never have shot a free-throw. That's okay: Even if you currently can make 80% of your free-throws on a consistent basis (results which would rank you in the top 10 to 15% of professional basketball players, by the way), I can make you better.

So, here's what I promise: If you follow these simple steps you'll be a good free-throw shooter.

Why can I make that promise? Using the same techniques I once made 750 free- throws in a row. (That's why 750 is a nice round number.)

And here's a bonus: If you follow the same process to break down any process into simple, repeatable, reliable steps...you'll become a better leader and run a better business. No matter how much the game changes, or how much technology changes the business environment, there is no need to reinvent the wheel—in basketball or in business.

I approach business the same way I approach free-throw shooting. The key is to turn a seemingly complex process into component parts that are much simpler and easy to understand. By stripping out the unnecessary and focusing on the basics, even the toughest goals can be accomplished.

Of course that doesn't mean you won't have to put in a lot of hard work and effort...but the last time I looked there are no shortcuts to any place worth going. Many people want to be great players. In fact, how many kids pick up a basketball hoping to sit the bench? Great players come through in the clutch. Great players want the ball when the game is on the line. When the game is close, great players are on the floor.

At times otherwise great players are not on the floor when the game is close, simply because they can't shoot free-throws. If you were able to choose, who do you want on the floor at the end of a close game? Do you want a Shaquille O'Neal, a 50% free-throw shooter, or a Ray Allen, an outstanding shooter with a career free-throw shooting percentage of nearly 90%?

As a coach, I'll take a Ray Allen any day. If a player can't make free-throws, I can't afford to have him on the floor at the end of close games. It's that simple. That's why teams make strategic substitutions to ensure shooters are on the floor at key moments. Take a look at statistics. The team that misses the most free-throws normally loses the game. The average game is decided by five or six points—or less. A team that misses six or eight free-throws typically loses the game. It's that simple.

Whoever makes the most free- throws tends to win.

The business team that executes reliably, even under adverse conditions, usually wins.

So let's start with a basic premise. First, the good news: There are only four ways to miss when you shoot a basketball.

You can miss:

◀ Long

◀ Short

◀ Left

◀ Right

That's it: There are only four ways to miss.

Here's the better news: All great shooters shoot the ball *the same way*.

That's right: All great shooters shoot the same way. You can miss in four different ways, but you only have to learn to shoot one way. (Want to talk best practices? Here you go.) Follow the example set by great shooters and you can become at the very least a good shooter. Regardless of your athletic ability or physical skills, if you practice the fundamentals and put in the work you can easily become a good shooter.

But what if you want to be a great shooter? What is the difference between a good shooter and a great shooter?

The difference in a good shooter and a great shooter is, oh, about a million shots. Practice is everything.

Focused repetition turns good shooters with good fundamentals into great shooters. Good shooters practice. Great shooters practice *extensively*. When I was young I shot several hundred free-throws a day. In fact, I wouldn't leave the gym each day until I had made 100 straight free-throws. (Before I became a great shooter, living up to that personal pledge made for some very long days.)

First we'll eliminate two variables: Missing right and left. If you practice the fundamentals and as a result start straight, finish straight, start in balance, and finish in balance—half your problems are eliminated: You will never miss to the right or to the left. While achieving that level of consistency is not easy, it can be done. Then we'll work on ensuring you don't shoot short or long.

So let's get to work!

Step One: Start straight to finish straight

If you have played basketball, you probably noticed that at the center of the free-throw line is a nail (or other small mark) indicating the point equidistant from both ends of the free throw line. If you draw a straight line from that mark to the rim, the line will split the middle of the rim. The nail indicates the center point. See Drawing A.

So, if you are like most people, you place your feet so they straddle the line.

If you do, you've already made a fundamental mistake.

Do this instead. If you are right-handed, place your right foot so the center mark lines up with the middle toe of your right foot, 1/2" behind the line. Then raise your arm and point your index finger at the center of the rim. By placing your foot in that position you will have created a straight line running from your shoulder through your arm and finger to the center of the rim. If you are left-handed, place your left foot so the mark lines up with the middle toe of your left foot.

Now you are lined up properly. You are in the basic position required to start straight.

Here's why: If you straddle the center mark on the foul line, your shoulder and arm will naturally be offset by as much as a foot or so from the center of the rim. Why shoot from an off-center position when you can just as easily center yourself? Becoming a great shooter is a matter of doing a number of little things well, and where you stand is the first of the little things you will do well.

Now move your left foot (or right foot, if you're left-handed) so your feet are shoulder-width apart. Both feet should face directly forward. Don't place either foot at an angle.

Now you're straight—and you're perfectly lined up with the rim.

Step Two: Grip the ball properly

First a question: What is the last part of your body that touches the ball when you shoot?

If your technique is sound, your middle and index fingers are the last parts of your body to touch the ball. That's why your next step is to grip the ball properly.

Just like lining up your feet, you will always grip the ball in the same place and in the same way. (Like everything else in the process, there are a million *wrong* ways but only one *right* way to grip a basketball.)

Your goal is to place your middle finger in the center of the ball—that way the ball will come out of your hand straight every time. Fortunately finding the center is easy. If you have a Wilson ball, place your middle finger so it lines up with the "l" in Wilson. If you have a Spalding basketball, your middle finger should line up with the "ld" in Spalding.

The manufacturers were nice enough to create a simple guide to the centerline of the ball—why not use it?

Then place your fingertips in the grooves of the ball, not on the pebbled surface itself. The grooves provide a better, more reliable grip.

Finally, place your thumb on the ball so you create a gap between the palm of your hand and the ball. The pad of your hand (just below your fingers) should touch the ball, but your palm should not. In fact, you should be able to take your other hand and put your fingers between the ball and the palm of your hand. Leave a little space.

Again, the key is to grip the ball the same way every time. Your goal is to eliminate as many variables as possible, and ball grip is a major variable. Grip the ball correctly and you've overcome a major source of variation; grip the ball incorrectly and you will introduce variation you cannot reliably overcome.

Step Three: Assume an Athletic Position

Once your feet are lined up, shoulder-width apart, and the ball is gripped properly, it's time to prepare to shoot.

First, bend your knees. At this point you only want a little bit of flex, say about an inch; if you bend your knees too far you won't have any room left to bend as you shoot the ball. Stick your butt back slightly so your head is a little bit in front of your hips.

You should not be standing straight: Stand with your knees flexed, butt out, head slightly forward of your hips. The athletic position helps keep you in balance at all times.

If it helps you to visualize the right position, imagine you're playing football and are about to tackle a runner. You would naturally get in an athletic position with your knees bent, butt out, head up, perfectly balanced, ready to attack and drive forward.

NOTE: The drawing below shows a straight line from the shooters right foot to the right knee to the right hip, to the right shoulder to the ball. This is very important in starting straight and finishing straight with the dot on the floor being the center point.

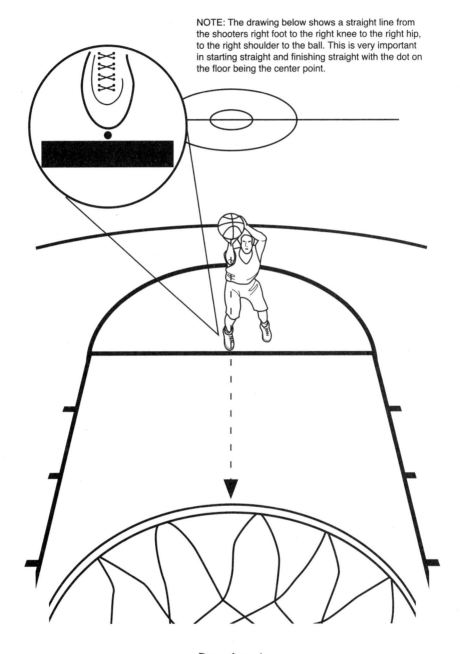

Drawing A

Or picture a fielder in baseball; they also assume an athletic position.

Step Four: Load...

Let's review:

◀ Feet properly aligned, shoulder width apart

◀ Ball gripped with the middle finger in the center-line, fingertips in the grooves

◀ Body in an athletic position

Now place your non-shooting hand on the side of the ball so you can extend your shooting arm forward. Turn your shooting hand so it faces flat to the floor while still gripping the ball properly. Your other hand will help hold the ball. Then bring your shooting hand straight back so it lines up with your shoulder.

Once thing you should notice immediately is that as you bring your shooting hand back, your elbow will stay close to your body so your arm can fold back into place. (In fact, your elbow should be close to if not slightly touching your side.)

That's great: If your elbow is out, the ball will roll off the side of your hand when you take your non-shooting hand off the ball. Try it: Once your shooting hand is back in position, close to your shoulder, let go of the ball with the other hand. You'll know right away if you are in the proper position because the ball will stay perfectly balanced in your hand. In the right position, you are balanced and the ball is balanced.

Once you have the ball in the shooting position, let the ball drop to the floor, leaving your hand and elbow in the shooting position. You should be able to touch your shoulder with your shooting hand, touch your hip with your elbow and extend your arm straight down to touch your knee. If you are not able to do all of these things, you do not have the ball set up properly.

If you are able to do these things, you are in the perfect shooting position.

The biggest mistake players make when shooting free-throws—other than setting their feet incorrectly or improperly gripping the ball—is to lower the ball from their shoulder down to their chest or even to their waist before they shoot. Once you are in the shooting position, the ball should stay in that position. Don't drop it down and then bring it back up. The ball should stay in place and your elbow should stay in.

You'll see why in a moment.

Step Five: And Fire

Now you're ready to shoot.

Where should you look? Your focus should be on the front of the rim. Not the back of the rim, not the backboard, not the crowd or your girlfriend or players on the other team...your focus should be on the front of the rim because that's where great shooters look.

The rest is easy: Bend your knees, drop down smoothly, come up smoothly, extend your shooting arm, and finish on your toes. Everything should go down together and come back up together. When you bend your knees, go down six or seven inches. Using your legs helps you keep your arm motion consistent. Your shot should be one fluid motion. Plus, if you shoot using mostly your arm and wrist, you will quickly get tired.

If you use your legs you can shoot free-throws all day. (I know—I've done it.)

Make sure you remain in an athletic position the entire time to ensure you stay in balance. If you bring your butt forward and straighten up, even slightly, you will lose balance and some amount of control over your shot. Plus, when you straighten up every shot you take is likely to be short—or you will have to over-compensate by using your arms more than you should.

Think of poor free-throw shooters you have seen. Many end up leaning forward or even taking a step forward after they shoot...good free-throw shooters finish in balance. In fact, they look like they are instantly ready to shoot again. Balance is critical.

Now let's talk trajectory.

When you shoot a ball, you must shoot with the proper trajectory. While it may not look like it, a regulation rim will hold two balls, side by side, with room to spare. The higher you shoot the ball, the more of the diameter of the rim you have available to you. Think of it this way: Hold a dinner plate in front of you. When the plate is parallel to you, it appears to be fairly large. Now slowly tilt the plate away from you. The more you tilt it, the smaller the surface area of the plate appears. When the plate is perpendicular to you, all you can see is the edge—in effect the plate has become a lot smaller.

The same is true in basketball. The "flatter" your shot the less margin available for error. Shooting with a flat trajectory provides significantly less margin for error. Shoot high and the ball fits easily into the rim; shoot flatter and it's a lot tougher. Shoot with little or no trajectory and your shot has to be nearly perfect.

Most players don't shoot high enough, which is unfortunate since in some cases a higher trajectory can almost double the chances of making a shot compared to using a flatter trajectory. Since two balls will fit in the rim, doesn't it make sense to take advantage of the diameter of the rim so the ball arcs down towards the rim?

It does make sense, but again, most players don't shoot high enough. (Partly I think that is because they don't think about the basic geometry involved.)

Here's a simple rule of thumb: For every ten feet you stand away from the basket, your shot should have a four-foot trajectory. That means shooting from the free-throw line requires a 17.5 foot trajectory.

Fortunately you don't need to be a mathematician to determine the optimal trajectory. By shooting with your legs, you will naturally shoot the ball higher because as you straighten your legs the motion will drive your body up and not forward. Simply flex down, flex up, in one fluid motion, and finish on your toes in an athletic position. Don't step forward, sideways, or backwards. Finish on your toes, in balance, arm extended, and the ball will naturally follow a high trajectory. Geometry will be your friend, but you won't have to think about it. Proper fundamentals will take care of the math for you.

If you feel your trajectory is too flat, correcting the arc is easy: Drop down farther by bending your knees before you shoot to generate a little more power. In fact, whether you shoot from two feet, from the free-throw line, or from behind the three-point line, everything that happens from your waist up should remain consistent. Your legs determine your shot. Power, distance, arc…it's all created by your legs. Great shooters use a lot of leg action, finishing high in the air on a jump shot or on their toes (but still balanced) on a free- throw.

As you release the ball, the last parts of your body that touch the ball should be your middle and index fingers. Because you use your legs to generate power, your release point will actually be upwards instead of outwards. (That's why great shooters finish with their shooting hand in the "goose neck" position: Arm up, palm flat, fingers dangling forward.)

The direction your index and middle fingers point when you follow through is the direction the ball will travel. If you follow through with your fingers to the right, your shot will go right. Finish with your fingers pointing left, even slightly, and your shot will go left.

Put it all together and you have shot the perfect free-throw. Bend, rise, release off your middle and index fingers…swish.

The easy part of shooting the perfect free-throw is setting up properly so you start straight and finish straight.

It's only slightly more difficult to grip the ball properly. It's only a little harder to maintain an athletic position and to finish in balance.

The hardest part of shooting the perfect free-throw is to modify your leg bend so you shoot with the right trajectory and the right distance. It's also hard, at least at first, to finish your shot with your fingers pointing directly at the basket and with your elbow in.

But anyone—and I do mean anyone—can overcome those challenges. I once coached 7th grade teams. I told them—as I've told you—that if they made their free-throws we would win the majority of our games. They bought in to my premise, and as a team we averaged 83% from the free-throw line, a result which would have put us, as a team, in the top five in the NBA in terms of free-throw percentage.

And we won city championships for five straight years. If 7th graders can shoot the perfect free-throw, so can you.

Simple Solutions to Common Problems

The most common problem people have is keeping their elbow in line with their shoulder and wrist as they shoot. Here's a simple drill to help you overcome this issue.

Get a ball and stand with your right shoulder touching a wall. (Your body should be perpendicular to the wall so you are looking down the wall instead of at the wall or away from the wall.) Grip the ball properly, bring your hand to your shoulder, and shoot straight up the wall. If your elbow is out it will hit the wall. With a few repetitions you will learn to keep your elbow in and you'll stop hitting the wall.

Or, get set at the foul line, feet shoulder width apart, knees slightly flexed, and before you bend your legs farther, drop the ball and let it roll off your hand. Bring your hand back up to your shoulder, down to your knee...and your elbow should hit your hip. If you drop your elbow and you don't hit your hip, your elbow is out of line. Practice the motion until it's easy to keep your elbow in line.

One other common problem involves a shooter's release point. When you shoot with the ball coming off your middle and index fingers, you naturally create a reverse rotation on the ball. If your fingers are perfectly centered and your hand and elbow are in perfect alignment, the rotation will also be perfect. But it's tough to determine whether the rotation is slightly off-axis, so here's an easy way to tell.

Grab a roll of white tape. Start by covering the center of the name of the manufacturer with the tape and wrap it around the center of the ball. (The tape should begin and end at the "l" in Wilson, for example.) When you shoot, the ball will spin and the tape will show you the nature of the ball's rotation. If the ball rotates slightly to the right, your shot is not coming off your middle and index fingers. The same thing is true if it rotates slightly to the left.

Your goal is to shoot so the ball does not appear to wobble as it sails towards the basket. Tape creates the perfect visual aid to ensure you develop a consistent, dead-on release point.

The Most Important Ingredient

Now you know the fundamentals. You know *how* to shoot the perfect free-throw, but there is still one thing missing.

The most important ingredient is confidence. Not cockiness; confidence. Confidence is when you *know* you will succeed, not because of ego or false pride but because you know through practice and repetition that you can and will make the shot.

Say it's a close game and I get fouled. When I go to the line, I know I'll make the shots—regardless of the score, regardless of a hostile crowd, in spite of any fear of letting my team down.

Why? I know I'll make the shot because I've made the same shot thousands and thousands of times. I don't have to worry about fundamentals. I don't have to worry about nerves. I don't have to worry about letting my team down. I don't have to worry because I've made the same shot thousands and thousands of times.

All I have to do is take a breath and think, "I've made this shot thousands of times. There's nothing to it. Set my feet, get in balance, elbow in, use my legs, release with my guide fingers pointing to the target… nothing to it."

Start playing the fight song and warm up the bus—the ball is going in the basket.

I've made the shot thousands of times.

Confidence also comes from following a set routine. By routine I don't mean personal quirks, like bouncing the ball ten times before I shoot, or spinning it several times, or kissing my fingers or tapping my chest with my fist. Those actions, theoretically, look cool (to some people, I guess; they don't look cool to me) but those actions do not in any way contribute to making free-throws. In game conditions you get ten seconds to shoot—why waste time doing anything that is non-essential?

Also, think about this. Go to YouTube and check out videos of great shooters. The NBA all-time leaders in free throw percentage include:

- Mark Price
- Rick Barry
- Steve Nash
- Calvin Murphy
- Scott Skiles
- Reggie Miller
- Larry Bird
- Peja Stojakovic
- Ray Allen

Check them out. None of them—*not one*—plays with the ball or performs odd rituals. They just shoot. (Note: Rick Barry used an underhand motion to shoot free-throws. He was often mocked for doing so, but the results he achieved are indisputable. Take a few minutes and watch his technique: He started straight, assumed an athletic position, and released the ball so it had a high trajectory and perfect rotation...other than shooting underhanded, his free-throw technique was almost identical to the fundamentals I have described.) Rick Barry wasn't concerned with how he looked at the free-throw line; he focused on results.

Since he is the second all-time free-throw shooter in NBA history, I think focusing on results paid off for him.

You don't need to perform odd rituals. Rituals cause you to think about something other than shooting the ball. Relying on rituals is also a sign of a lack of confidence. You don't need a ritual to help you make the shot. You need fundamentals, lots of practice, and real confidence based on the knowledge you've made the shot hundreds and thousands of times.

When you shoot free-throws, you step up to the line to make free-throws, not to "look good" for the crowd. Adding any elements that distract or in some small way increase your chances for failure is, frankly, stupid.

You want to look good? Make the shot. Success *always* looks good.

A few years ago I worked with a high school player and helped him become a 90% free-throw shooter. His fundamentals were spot-on. He went to college and I noticed he stopped shooting the same way. I asked him why, and he said, "We're on TV a lot now...and I didn't think I looked very cool."

His priority was no longer making shots—his priority was looking cool.

And his game suffered.

Why do something that doesn't work? There are two basic ways to learn, in basketball, in business, and in life:

1. Find a person who is successful, and do what he or she does

2. Find a person who is not successful, and don't do what he or she does

If your favorite player is not a good free-throw shooter...don't shoot the way he does!

That's true in basketball and in business.

All great shooters shot the same way. You may want to reinvent the wheel, especially if you think it makes you look cool or helps you express yourself as an individual, but in reality you won't be able to successfully reinvent the wheel. Ray Allen free-throws may not look cool to some people...but at the end of a close game every coach wants a Ray Allen on the floor. Every true fan wants a Ray Allen on the floor, too.

Ray Allen doesn't worry about looking cool; Ray Allen just wants to win. Good employees don't worry about looking cool or expressing their individuality; they just want to help the company succeed. Unless you're a model or actor, looking cool has nothing to do with success. Success comes from knowing what you want and doing what it takes to get what you want.

So here is the routine I follow. You should too. Get the ball, set your feet, grip the ball properly, bend your knees about one inch and assume an athletic position, bring the ball back to your shoulder with your elbow in, drop down, rise, extend, shoot the ball high enough so it arcs down towards the basket, finish with your index and middle fingers pointing at the center of the basket—swish. Once I am set, my only thought is to place my middle and index finger inside the front of the rim as I follow through.

No muss, no fuss, no extras...efficient and effective.

Once you have the fundamentals down, the remaining key to success is practice. But not just any kind of practice; focused practice. A few years ago I was chatting with a prominent Division I basketball coach. We were discussing different strategies for closing out close games. I mentioned that his players were not, as a team, particularly good free-throw shooters, and gently suggested his team should spend more time working on free-throws in practice. He said, "We work on that all the time. My kids shoot between 50 and 100 free-throws every practice."

I said, "I'm sure they do...but your kids' fundamentals are off. They may be shooting lots of free-throws, but their technique is off. They are *shooting* free-throws but they are not *working* on their free-throw shooting technique."

It was clear he felt simply shooting lots of free-throws was enough.

I disagree completely with that approach. If your fundamentals are flawed and you practice using poor technique...you actually reinforce poor techniques and become a worse shooter, not a better shooter. Learn the fundamentals first—then practice using those fundamentals so the right techniques are reinforced. What's the old saying? Practice doesn't make perfect; *perfect* practice makes perfect.

While this sounds a little harsh, think of it this way: If you motivate an idiot, all you have a motivated idiot. If you practice shooting using poor techniques, you end up being a poor shooter. In basketball, and in business, establish the proper fundamentals first—then practice those fundamentals.

Practice for the sake of practice helps no one.

Okay, I can guess what you're thinking. Basketball is a complex, multi-faceted game, and free-throws are just one small part. Why so much focus on free-throws?

Picture you're a kid in high school. You play varsity basketball for two years. That's about twenty-five games a year, a total of approximately fifty games. If you go to the basket a number of times during each game you'll get fouled on a consistent basis. A decent player can easily take the ball inside eight to ten times a game. Maybe you miss the layup…but more likely you either make the shot or get fouled. Both are great outcomes.

If you draw a foul, three good things happen: An opposing player picks up a foul, your team moves closer to being in the bonus, and you get to shoot free-throws. If you are an 80% free-throw shooter, you will score between 600 and 800 points during your high school career just from shooting free-throws alone. Add in a reasonable amount of points from the floor and you'll easily join the 1,000-point club, placing you in pretty exclusive company.

Or think of it another way. In 2009–2010 Kevin Durant won the NBA scoring title with 30.1 points per game. Not only is he an amazing scorer, but he is also a superb free-throw shooter: He averaged 90% from the free-throw line. He shot an average of nine free-throws per game.

LeBron James ended the season second on the scoring list, averaging 29.7 points per game. He finished .4 points per game behind Durant.

LeBron is an amazing scorer, but he only averaged 74% from the line. Compared to other NBA players a 74% free-throw average certainly isn't bad, but think about the difference between LeBron James and Kevin Durant. LeBron gets to the foul line on average more than ten times a game. I can easily argue that becoming a better free- throw shooter would add two to four additional points per game to LeBron's scoring average. If he had been an 80% free throw-shooter he would have won the NBA scoring title.

It gets worse. The Cavaliers lost eight games by three points or less. If LeBron was an 85% free-throw shooter, his team might have won several more games. If he was a 90% free-throw shooter, his team might have won five or six more games.

All because of free-throws: Not three-pointers, not jumpers, not dunks, but all because of free-throws.

Since most basketball games are fairly close, the same logic applies to any player. Make your free-throws and your team is much more likely to win. Teams that make free-throws win—it's that simple. Down the stretch those teams don't mind if the other team commits a lot of fouls; fouls lead to free points.

Also keep in mind what happens during a one-and-one situation. On non-shooting fouls, a player goes to the line and shoots a one-and-one. If he makes the first shot, he gets a second. If he misses the first shot and the opposing team gets the defensive rebound (which happens most of the time) then a scoring opportunity is lost. Miss the front end of a one-and-one and you not only give away the chance to score one point, you give away the chance to score a second point on the subsequent free-throw. Due to one-and-one free-throws, free-throw shooting statistics are slightly misleading because they don't account for the "opportunity cost" of a second free-throw when the first shot is missed.

Clearly LeBron is an incredible athlete. Nothing stops him from being a better free- throw shooter—well, nothing but poor fundamentals and a lack of focused practice.

Business is no different. Every successful business is based on a number of fundamental processes and proce- dures that must be performed correctly. For example, a superstar salesperson may bring in a major order . . . but if the shipping department delivers the order to the wrong address, the team still "loses." Every aspect of a basketball game is critical. Every aspect of your business is critical.

Again, the key is to focus and practice like you play. Jack Nicklaus was once asked why it took him so long to hit a bucket of balls on the practice range. He said, "Every shot I hit is a winning shot. I don't just walk up and hit. I approach every shot like it is life or death; if I don't practice that way, I won't be ready when the pressure is really on."

I started putting the pressure on when I was in my backyard (or was it in the Boston Garden?) I put pressure on myself. I pretended every shot was a game-winning shot. I didn't realize it at the time, but I was building a winning mental attitude. I pretended every shot was a buzzer-beater. I truly felt every shot *mattered*.

It paid off. In high school I made three straight game-winning shots. After the third game a reporter said, "You act like making those shots is nothing. After it goes in you appear to be the least excited guy on the floor. Why are you so matter of fact?"

I said, "Every shot I take is a game winner. That's how I practice and that's how I play. I expect to make the shot."

While I never became a great player, that is how great players practice. Every time they take a potential game-winning shot, great players don't feel the pressure because they have made millions of shots under pressure. Take how I shot free-throws: I had to make 100 straight in order to go home. Think about it: When you reach 20, it's no big deal. Make 50 in a row? No big deal. At 80 in a row, the pressure starts to build because at that point, who wants to start over? At 90 in a row there is even more pressure.

By 95 the pressure is on...but not really. When I reached 95 in a row all I had to do was remember I had just made 95 shots in a row—do the same thing and the ball will go in. In fact, I can't ever remember getting into the 90s and missing a shot. By then I was filled with confidence. If you make 90 in a row, why would you think you would miss the next shot? It's automatic. You're the man. Your track record says so.

Also, as you might recall from an earlier chapter, I put even more pressure on myself by making practice a lot harder. I used the device Coach Stern gave me to make the effective size of the rim much smaller. I had to do everything right in order for the ball to go in—it made practice a lot tougher, but it also increased my confidence in a real game. Compared to what I practiced on, the rim looked as big as a hula hoop. How could I miss?

One other fun thing about being a great free-throw shooter: You get called on in the clutch.

I loved when the other team committed a technical foul because I knew our coach would send me to the line. He chose me to represent our team. He counted on me. His faith in me gave me a real sense of pride and accomplishment.

So while I knew all eyes were on me—I knew I would come through.

Knowing you will come through—for your team or for your business—is an incredible feeling.

The Perfect Free-Throw: An Overview

1. Start straight and finish straight. Place your middle toe 1/2" behind the line on the nail at the center of the free-throw line, feet shoulder width apart, pointing straight at the basket.

2. Grip the ball with your middle and index finger centered on the manufacturer's name. Fingertips go in the grooves. Ball rests on your fingers and the pad of your hand, not your palm.

3. Get in an athletic position, knees bent about one inch, butt back, head up. Balance is everything.

4. Bring the ball straight back to your shoulder, elbow in.

5. Bend your legs, staying in athletic position with head behind hips, drive upwards, extend your shooting arm, and shoot the ball high. Remember: Never drop the ball from your shoulder as you shoot. Power comes from your legs, not your arms.

6. Finish on your toes, head in front of your hips, butt out, completely in balance, shooting hand in the goose neck position with your middle and index finger pointing at the center of the basket.

7. Do it again—thousands of times.

If you have questions, feel free to email me at rjfoley@ kc.rr.com I love turning good free-throw shooters into great free-throw shooters.

Who knows? 750 might be a nice round number for you, too.